JUNKIE
By Tommy Zee

Published by: Immortal Publishing
Po Box 162, Strasburg, Va 22657, U.S.A.

Edited by: Larry Jones- ltjones@gmail.com
Cover created by: Tommy Zee
Copyright © 2015 By Tommy Zee

All rights reserved. This book, or parts thereof, may not be reproduced in any form without permission in writing from the publisher,
Immortal Publishing, PO Box 162, Strasburg, Va 22657

The scanning, uploading and distribution of this book via the internet or via any other means without the permission of the author is illegal and punishable by law. Please purchase only authorized electronic editions, and do not participate in or encourage electronic piracy of copyrighted materials. Your support of the author's rights is appreciated. The publisher does not have any control over and does not assume any responsibility for author or third party websites or their content.

Library of Congress Control Number: 2015934812
ISBN e-book- 978-0-9961413-1-4
Print paperback- 978-0-9961413-0-7
Print hardback- 978-0-9961413-2-1

This book is dedicated to all addicts who have lost their lives to substance abuse. May you have voices beyond this world. May your lives tell stories and yield warnings to those questioning the path to follow in your footsteps.

Contents

Introduction 5
Childhood Mishaps 8
Bad Reputation 19
Cocaine = Cancer 26
Straight Edge Vs. Heroin Addict 34
Moving Into Insanity 39
Junkie Soul Mate 51
The House of Destruction 61
I Fought the Law 73
Fucking Everything up 79
What Have I Done? 94
Couldn't Stay Clean 101
Falling for a Monster 110
Why Did I Do it? 119
My Second Chance 124
Recovery 130
To the Addict 134
To the Affected Family 139
To Those who Find Sobriety 144

Introduction

I am a 25-year-old woman. I took my last drink and drug on March 29th, 2012. Since getting sober, the heroin epidemic has worsened. Whatever the substance, addiction is not going away. As 2015 draws to its midpoint, 23.5 million Americans are addicted. It is estimated that one in every 10 Americans over the age of 12 deal with addiction. It is likely that only 11 percent will get treatment. To me, this means most people have dealt with dependency issues. Whether it is a coworker, loved one or neighbor, it is safe to say that every person knows someone affected. Sharing my story may help you understand why. What does an addict think? Why did I do the things I did?

In the three years I have been clean, I buried 15 friends, all victims of overdoses. Children in a world without parents. A mother screaming in agony as her child's coffin, lifted by a crane, found its resting place six-feet under. Most young adults were finishing college, getting married, buying a house, having kids and starting their lives. I chose a more difficult path. I have seen and been through more at my age than most people will know in a lifetime. It is important you know that in no way am I trying to glorify addiction. This is an autobiography of my experience with addiction. I thought a life of partying with substances seemed fun and inviting. I so badly wanted to be like the famous girls who partied on MTV. What it turned out to be was nothing close to that idea.

My drug use left permanent medical damage. Due to the constant opiate overload in my brain, I suffer migraines that mimic a stroke. I am legally blind in my right eye due to one of these episodes. People may think the biggest consequence of addiction is death. I am an example that, even while sober, drug use can constantly remind you later of its permanent, physical damage.

Other than being an author, I am a hair designer and a public speaker. I have two brothers and an identical twin sister. My parents gave us an extremely privileged upbringing, and they love all of us unconditionally. I am sharing my story to raise awareness of addiction's consequences. Those of us trying to educate young people are upstaged by celebrities who glorify drug use. Perhaps if they paid earlier for their addictions, this would not be so. I think it takes celebrities longer to experience the consequences because they are cushioned by fame, allowing them a longer time to reach their bottom. When that bottom is reached, the crash can be pretty severe. Lots of merchandise and song lyrics make substance abuse sound attractive, but it is far from it.

I want you to know my attitude in addiction was arrogant. I truly believed nothing bad could ever happen to me. Perhaps I believed I was above, or better, than the homeless junkies begging on the street corner. Addiction is a sick and twisted demon. It attaches to you in a disgustingly permanent, and helpless, way. This is why few survive. Why parents are burying their children. Why children are growing up without parents. I will warn you my story is not pretty. It may make some feel uncomfortable. A privileged, pretty, smart girl, who was hopeful and had so much to offer, but ended up addicted to heroin. Homeless, jobless, a hollow shell of a human being, who destroyed herself over and over again.

If there is anything I hope you receive from this book, it is to refrain from abusing substances. Even if only one time, you will pay a consequence. May you stay true to yourself. Before a line has been crossed, you must set a boundary. Before you become a victim. Before you become another statistic. Before your family must cry at your funeral.

Childhood Mishaps

My sister, Ro, and I were born May 12, 1989, around noon. Our parents were ecstatic to have twins. My mother was 24, an amazingly beautiful woman. She immigrated to America at age 11 with her family from Israel. My father was a Los Angeles native, who was making his way as an auto technician. My parents met at a local car dealership where they both worked. They fell in love quickly and are still happily married today.

On October 5, 1992, my mother gave birth to a beautiful boy named Zack. He is a wild one. Riding dirt bikes since age 5, he became a welder at 17 and a fabricator at 21. He loves extreme sports and being active. On Friday the 13th of March 1998, she gave birth to a second son, Emmet. He has always been extremely smart. Emmet knows amazing, intricate facts in all kinds of matters. Whether it be political, scientific or physiological, he is very educated. He started riding his BMX bike at the age of 3. He earned his first sponsor at age 12. In 2014, he traveled to France where he parlayed a first-ever trick and became a world-renowned athlete. He is a humble 16-year-old, always positive and smiling.

When Ro and I were 14 months old, my mother hired Berta, a nanny to help her. She was an older woman from Guatemala. She was elegant, always wearing pretty skirts and looking well put together. She did not know much English, so we learned Spanish. She had left behind a family of her own, to come to the United States where she could make a better living and send money back to her children. As we grew older, she would walk us to and from our elementary school. She made us dinner and helped with the household chores. She was our second mother. She taught us morals and values while loving us unconditionally. I loved her very much.

I was nine. Ro, Zack, Berta and I were playing hockey in the driveway. We used a small, orange ball instead of a puck. One day, Berta stepped on the ball, rolled backwards and fell onto her wrist. A broken wrist, a cast and a possible lawsuit sparked a feud between her family and ours. My mother had no choice but to let her go. I remember that morning so clearly. My mother woke us up. She told us we would be going downstairs to say goodbye to our nanny of almost nine years. I felt robbed. It was hard to breathe, like someone had punched me in the chest. It was the first time I felt an emotional hurt that was so overbearing. I could not comprehend how my mother could expect me to willingly give up a woman I loved so much. She was much more than a nanny. She was my best friend. My confidante. A life without her was something I could not picture. She was part of our family. What kind of family would just remove one of its most important members?

Resentfully, I marched down the stairs. It seemed unreal, unfair and wrong. Berta stood there, trying to keep herself composed. Her brother and sister-in-law waited at the bottom of the driveway. I tried to find words, but felt short of breath in trying to accept the situation. I was so angry my blood was boiling. When I hugged her, we both cried. I wanted to hold onto her and never let her go. After a few moments, she pulled back and kissed my forehead. She told me to be good and to mind my parents. I knew once she pulled away, things would never be the same. Something as simple as hugging my nanny would no longer be possible. She was leaving our family and our home. There was talk of us visiting later, but when we embraced, we both knew this was for the last time. It was terrible, and the pain was surreal. I longed for something I could no longer have, a relationship I needed. It was the moment in a child's life when she discovers there is evil in the world. It was a cold and debilitating disappointment. She said her goodbyes to the rest of the family and walked to her brother's car. Unfortunately, we have not seen each other since.

I had never cried like that before. I could not retch out a sob horrible enough to describe my pain. If I was older, I would go live with her. I would stop this. I stood in the front yard and watched her as she was driven away. Forever. I ran past my parents. Those evil, selfish, heartless beings who had taken my Berta away. I hated them.

I was too young to understand that Berta's sister-in-law had threatened an exploitive lawsuit against my parents for Berta's injury. When my parents consulted their lawyer, he told them it could get very ugly. That every day she continued to be with us, she was a liability. If something else happened, and they won the suit, we could lose our house. My parents had to protect our family, but as a small child, it was too much to comprehend. I ran up to the room that Berta had lived in for so long. It was empty and desolate. All that remained was a full-size bed and some little objects. The bed wore a comforter with colorful buttons on it. I curled up onto the bed and cried my eyes out for hours. I did not, and could not, get rid of the pain. She was gone, and I took it personally. I felt like I was being punished. I wondered if Berta even loved us at all. Surely, she must have fought to stay. She could not willingly walk away from us like she did not love us. I depended on her and looked forward to seeing her every day. Now she would simply be absent from my life. My heart was broken, and I did not feel myself. My life as I knew it would be different, and I absolutely hated that it had to be this way.

Still now, there is a dull pain in my chest when I talk about her, and I rarely do. It felt like she had passed away, and I was mourning her death. It never stopped hurting, but with time, I accepted it as reality. That nothing could change it, and I had to accept the pain for the loved one I had lost. I stayed in her room for three days. My parents allowed me to have the room, hoping I would better cope with the situation. I lived in that room until I moved into my own apartment later in life. My youngest brother lives in there now.

Sometimes I wonder if my siblings and parents remember her the way I do, or if they think of her as often I do. I sometimes want to write her and tell her how I miss her. I am afraid, though, in her old age she may not remember me, which would be devastating.

This incident kindled the fire raging inside me. The flame of hatred and anarchy. The urge to seek revenge on those who had wronged me. And the painful feelings which overcame me. It was then I knew I would sell my soul to stop an emotional pain so consuming.

When I was around the age of four, we had an awful car accident. It was my mother's birthday, and we were leaving the lake after a long weekend of fun. We packed our minivan and readied for the long trip home. My uncles and aunts did the same and left shortly after we did. Early into the drive, my mother undid her seat belt to get a pillow from the backseat. Her window was down. My father hit a patch of sand, and the van swerved out of control. The van started to roll, and my mother went flying out the window. My father tried to grab her, but she slipped from his grasp. Our van rolled over six times. My brother Zack, barely a year old, was unharmed. My father had minor cuts and bruises. Ro had a hip injury from her seat belt buckle, unable to walk until it healed. I had been sleeping with my head resting against the door; my head and face becoming a pin-cushion of protruding glass when the window exploded. Our injured bodies were placed on beach towels by the side of the road. A few, kind people had stopped to help until the paramedics arrived. There was a beautiful woman who sat above me and gently removed some shards from my face. She kept telling me how beautiful I was and used a Popsicle to apply ice to my swollen face. I could not see either of my parents. One of my uncles had driven to the scene, and I could see him putting my brother into his car. I kept asking where my mother was. No one answered.

My father went looking for her, not knowing what he would find. He was determined to find her. She was far from the accident scene, lying in the desert sand. Her body was crooked and awkward. Her bones seemed out of place. He told her she was badly injured and moving her was risky. He sat and talked to her until the helicopter arrived. My mother had broken her neck and would be in a metal halo for close to a year. She also broke her wrist, shattered her elbow and had broken a few other bones.

The accident took a toll on our family. We twins had to support each other, even at age four. Zack feared the sight of my mom; the halo was intimidating. She recovered from her injuries and gave birth to Emmet, our last family member, a few years later. Today she suffers from lupus and migraines. Her unique case of lupus is possibly related to her injuries as the disease does not run in our family. She is in good health, and we collectively do whatever we can to keep her comfortable and happy.

At the age of 12, I went to a two-week, sleep-away summer camp. We traveled by bus from California to Utah. I met a cute boy who was in the older group. We decided to be in a relationship after the first few days of meeting one another. I should have been having fun with the other campers my age, but I was precocious and always pushing it, getting into things that seemed dangerous. I liked the thrill of doing things I knew I should not. Being so young, I had never had a boyfriend before and thought being in a relationship meant holding hands, maybe even a kiss on the lips, but no more than that. About five days into the trip, the counselors were away staging a ceremony for other campers. Those of us who stayed behind were supposed to be sleeping. I decided to hang out with my boyfriend and the older kids. He became very pushy about the idea of lying down with him. I felt trapped. I wanted to run away, but I was paralyzed with fear. If I refused, maybe he would not think I was cool anymore. Perhaps he would humiliate me in front of others. I decided lying down would be all right.

I went with him, and he got aggressive. I realized he was not tired, and his intention was not to go to sleep. At first I pretended I wanted to be there. Then I became overwhelmed. I was afraid and felt threatened. I tried to leave, but he pulled me back into the tent. He was angry and much stronger than me. I was raped that night—for the first time. Afterward, I stumbled back to my own tent, too petrified to close my eyes. I sat awake until morning when I began vomiting and shaking. The stress from the trauma was affecting me physically. I could not hold food down, and I stopped talking. The camp staff became worried and did their best to get me to eat. There was no witness to the attack. This boy told me what happened was common in relationships, and he made me feel stupid and immature for crying and trying to stop him. I was too afraid to tell anyone what happened because I felt as if I had done something wrong. I finally told an older girl. She told me it was normal, that even though it was scary and felt wrong, I had to keep it to myself, and eventually I would get used to it. I found out later this girl had been sexually abused by her stepfather, which was where her misguided advice came from.

A few days later we went on a hike. My starvation and dehydration caught up to me. I passed out somewhere along the trail. I remember being placed on a picnic table and waiting for the paramedics. I could hear everyone around me, but I was unable to wake up completely. I just wanted to go home. When I finally opened my eyes, I could see my attacker starting to panic. He knew if I went to the hospital, I would tell them what happened. So I refused to go. I let the paramedics tend to me there on the table. I knew if I went to the hospital, there was a chance they could see the bruises and would realize something was wrong. I did not want my family to find out, so I told them I was afraid of hospitals, and I wanted to stay with the camp.

The camp staff called my parents and made me speak with my father. I told him I could not eat because the food was gross. I never told my parents what happened. When I got home, I started listening to dark music and blaming myself. What happened weighed heavily on me. It did not feel right at all. I felt as if my innocence was stripped away. While I did not know much about sex, I found it troubling that this is what you were left feeling like after. I wondered if everyone felt this way and how anyone could consider it enjoyable. The boy and I kept in touch by phone, but soon after we returned home, he was arrested. We never spoke again. I felt so guilty and ashamed. I had so much hatred in my heart. I felt ruined. My innocence and virginity had been robbed from me, but I took my fellow camper's advice not to tell anyone about the attack.

The emotional pain was so overbearing, I turned to physical pain. I began burning myself. Sometimes I used accelerants such as nail polish remover. Having control of my physical pain helped distract me from the emotional madness in my head. The other kids at school thought I was weird. I had a hard time connecting with people because I was afraid of them. It was that night I saw the evil and violence of which mankind was capable. Now that I knew how easily I could be taken advantage of, it was hard to avoid isolation. It was a fear so stark I could not keep it out of my mind. I perceived everyone differently from that day forward. I recognize it even now, the hair on my neck standing up when random strangers look at me as a piece of meat. I can feel their obscene presence picturing dirty thoughts about me as they stand behind me in line at the store. I know these same ideas live inside everyone, to a point.

I found a girl in middle school who understood me. She was a bit off, like me. The same piece of her seemed missing, although she had been molested as a child. We were young, broken girls who looked normal to most outsiders. We shared the same illness, that of fearing the evil inside others. Knowing that those who are sicker than others will act on it. That, in a moment, we could be their next victims. We could be assaulted again. No one and nothing could protect us, and most of the world did not even worry about these possibilities. She had something I did not, a cure to silence the insanity in our minds. To quiet the fear that overcame us. This girl introduced me to the power of substances. Starting with nicotine and alcohol, then graduating to morphine. In those moments of ecstasy, these poisons reacted in my body. The fear was gone. The weight was lifted, and I was not a prisoner of fear any longer.

I had longed for her, and she had helped me. She understood me. I had to spend time with her, to share the poison, to feel normal. I relied on her as much more than a friend. She was my keeper. If I was not with her, I had to bear the pain and disappointment. I needed to be with her as much as possible. I became addicted to her company and her access to drugs. My mother grew weary of this friendship. In fear, I ended up telling my mother about the morphine, and my friend was caught stealing. I was not allowed to see her again, but I was not worried. Now, I knew there were other people in the world like me. They had access to what I needed to numb the pain. Just like I found her, I would find another. My demon of addiction had found me. From then on, we sought those who were as sick as we were. For years, I chased the high in order to furnish my craving for substance. As time went on, I was not a little girl anymore. I was a slave to death and despair, and I was in love with this thought. I found a way to avoid dealing with the horrible things I had braved. I knew then that I would do anything for the drug, and no one could stop me.

Bad Reputation

Throughout middle school my friends were inconsistent as I had a hard time fitting in. Most of my friends had known me from elementary school, but they were busy focusing on academics. In high school, I hung out with a small group of guys. Ro was dating a guy who said he was in a gang and had some pretty shady friends. She hung out with Hispanic girls who were known to be involved with gangs and other sketchy people. Things became dangerous when her group of friends turned against her. Her best friend resented her because she was Caucasian and lived in a nice house. Her envy grew, and she convinced the group that my sister was not a friend, but an enemy.

First, they pulled a knife on her in the girl's locker room. The school also feared these girls and their families, making the administration hesitant to take action against them. When the incident with the knife occurred, the school cited a lack of witnesses, saying my sister was over-exaggerating. The group of girls was told to leave my sister alone, and the principal guaranteed my sister's safety to my parents.

Shortly after this episode, things turned worse. One of my friends came running at lunch, shouting my sister had been jumped. I ran to Ro, who was crying and beaten. I did my best to comfort her and examine the damage. These girls had ripped her fingernails off, punched her braces through her lips and caused her nose to bleed. I was so infuriated I wanted to kill them. I had never seen Ro so vulnerable; she had been attacked and no one tried to help her. She was physically hurt and emotionally crushed.

They only took the group's main instigator to the office. Our parents were called, and the police came. My sister stood her ground and managed to punch most of the girls at least once. The officer informed my parents that during school hours, there is no such thing as self-defense. Because my sister had also hit some of the girls, this was considered a fight, not an attack. Both girls were placed under arrest. My mother was furious. When my mother questioned why the other girls involved were not in trouble, the principal told her there was no proof that more than one girl was involved, despite the fifty-plus students who watched the fight. He then informed her that my sister and I would have to leave the high school. His reasoning was if he expelled all the girls involved, it would make the school look questionable. They let me finish out the semester, and Ro was home-schooled until the next semester started. We went to another high school in a neighboring town, close to my mother's work. My mother filed a complaint with the school district about the incident, and shortly after, the principal lost his job.

I was very anxious to be at the new school. No one knew me, which meant I could be anyone I wanted. This town was known for being wealthy, and I feared how we would fit in. Shortly into my first day, I found I already had a reputation. It was like a game of telephone. There was a story that my sister and I were violent and had been expelled for fighting. Some people were intrigued, others frightened. This rumor gave me an opportunity to be feared. I could re-create myself into something I was not. I could intimidate others with this false story. I had a new sense of control. I could pick who I wanted to be friends with, because if I did not like you, as the story went, I would kick your ass. I went along with it. I became obsessed with the ability to be someone I was not. Like most addicts, I wanted more and more.

In attempts to keep up with my bad reputation, I would need some scary friends. Intimidating people who other students stayed away from. I found the druggies and drug dealers of the school. The main bad boy, Stan, was supposedly unattainable. All the girls warned me that despite his magnetism, he never had a girlfriend and would not commit. I accepted the challenge, and we began a relationship. He was known for having laid-back parents who smoked weed with him, making his home a party house. If you needed marijuana or alcohol, you knew where to go. Every day there would be a different group of people, from the cheerleaders and football team, to the math geeks and punk kids. At school, they ignored us. They pretended they did not even know us; but when they needed a fix, we were the first ones they called. They all knew they could count on us to score drugs, booze or cigarettes. My best friend, Clair, and I became the bad girls in school. Clair was a tall girl, and built. She was not afraid of anyone or anything, and she could party harder than most guys.

Ro had a hard time making friends. I think after what had happened at the previous high school, it was hard for her to trust. She withdrew from others and focused on school with ambitions of becoming a nurse. At lunch, she would sit alone next to the trash can. Sometimes people would bully her. She was the nerd that no one understood. The smart kid who people picked on for lacking friends and valuing education. She would come home crying, and I knew how sad she was. I was her twin, and it was my job to always be her friend. To be loyal and dependable. But it did not matter. I was cool, and I had drugs. She became irrelevant. Our relationship began to wither away. We rarely even talked at home. She hated me and my friends. My friends were sometimes the ones who bullied her. I never told them to stop; a few times I even joined them. Anything to keep my access to drugs and my new friends. My addiction had become my priority, blinding me to the consequences of my actions. I did not need my twin anymore. I needed my friends, my addiction and the shallow lie of the life I was living.

My mother had a feeling I was doing bad things, but she had no proof. I was caught with cigarettes during my senior year and was grounded. I started to dislike school and stopped showing up. I would ditch after a class or two and make it back before my mother came to pick me up. Once I started driving, it was easier to lie about where I was. I attended every Saturday detention, except two, during my sophomore and junior years, and I was suspended three times. I always made sure my homework was turned in, and I showed up for all tests. This way my grades were kept up, and they could not expel me for attendance. I did not deserve to graduate, but I did. I had enough truancies to be expelled, but my mother worked closely with my counselor and vice-principal to ensure I could walk at graduation. Meanwhile, Clair ended up getting expelled and went to a high school in another town where her father lived. We continued to see each other, smoking weed, drinking and making trouble whenever possible.

Before I dated Stan, I was involved with a boy from a different school. While it did not last, I met some friends through him. One of them was Justin. Clair also knew him well. Justin was a very giving and kind person. He was concerned with the well-being of his friends and family. He was dependable and truly a treasure. One night, high on pills and sucked into depression, I decided to end my life. I told Justin how I was feeling via internet chat, and he called my mother and told her. My mom took my pills and sharp objects away, making it difficult to go through with my plan. At first, I resented Justin for being a tattletale, but I later appreciated that he valued my life enough to save it.

Before Stan, Clair and I bought weed from Justin, who enjoyed smoking as much as we did. On a weeknight in July, Clair called Justin for some weed and agreed to meet him at a local strip mall. I was out with my mom and agreed to meet them later. When I tried to contact them, their phones went to voicemail. I figured they were busy and went to bed. In the morning, Clair called. She was distraught. She told me she had been waiting for Justin in the parking lot and saw him crossing the street. A pill-popping driver failed to see him on his bicycle and hit him with her car. Justin was rushed to the hospital where he died.

I was 15 when I experienced the first death of a loved one, and the pain was unreal. Justin had been such a loyal friend and a kind person. He saved my life, and in a time where I may have been able to do something to save his, I was absent. I put the blame for his death on my shoulders. His funeral was beyond tragic, and his poor mother's pain was felt amongst the room's mourners. His lifeless body lay in a coffin, beside it, his motorcycle boots. The preacher told us how no one would ever be able to fill those boots again. I sat on the floor next to the casket with Justin's siblings and close friends. The mortuary played a video of his life, and we all held each other as we sobbed. After the service, I went up to the casket to see my dead friend. It was hardly Justin. The makeup the mortician used was not of natural skin color. I could see where they had tried to glue flesh wounds back together on his scalp. Once this was my friend, someone I could talk to all night. Someone who laughed and made me smile. Now I stood over his body. His eyes and mouth glued closed forever. He would never smile, or laugh ever again. I needed to say goodbye to him, and I did not want to. I bent over and kissed his forehead. I had never wondered what death felt like, but as my lips touched the cold, dead skin of my friend, I felt it. It was heavy and lonely. All I wanted was to crawl in the coffin with my friend and disappear forever. He did not deserve to lose his life, he deserved to live. And if it were not for him being a tattletale, our roles could have been reversed. It could have been him standing over my dead body in a coffin, and I much preferred that situation.

I think a small part of everyone in the mortuary died that day. In our early teenage years, we came to know we are not guaranteed tomorrow. Nothing in life was certain except for death, and we would experience much more in our lifetimes.

My ambition had always been to be a cosmetologist. Stan's mother did hair and would often teach me little things about cuts and color throughout high school. I experimented with my friends' hair and became passionate about pursuing a job in the hair industry. I could not wait to start beauty school. I enrolled as soon as I was able. There was a long waiting list, and my mother helped ensure I would begin shortly after high school graduation.

The following fall I started on the path to my career. I was excited, but soon learned I would face many obstacles. My addiction would be getting stronger and stronger. It would be waiting for the perfect opportunity to take precedence over my life, and I would allow it.

Cocaine = Cancer

In the fall of 2007, I walked into my first day of beauty school. I was eager to meet the other women. This was not like the small town in which I had grown up. It was the busy city of Los Angeles, with its wide diversity of people. I was the youngest in my class by five years. There was pretty, sweet Jesse, who was nearly my age. She was my only friend. Most of the other women were older. It seemed as if from the moment I met my peers, they would not accept me. There were only three levels in cosmetology school: freshman, junior and senior. The junior and senior classes were taught in a different building, which doubles as a salon, open to the public. We were assigned a workstation while attending theory classes in the morning.

Mondays were demonstration days where salons and product professionals showed what it was like to have a career in the beauty industry. School was far from easy. Classes were six hours a day with optional Saturday classes. The requirement was to complete 1,600 hours before qualifying for the state exam. There were also hundreds of practice procedures that had to be approved by instructors on a daily basis. The program was intimidating on its own, not to mention the pack of bickering, bullying women I had to fend off each day.

Being young, I did not know how to stand up for myself. When I went over to the junior floor, Jesse befriended the kennel of rabid women who hated me.

They often called me spoiled and tormented me in front of everyone. They would do anything to get to me and make sure I felt unwelcome, they went so far as to let the air out of the tires on my car. They would yip-yip names at me, snapping vulgar names from across the room. They growled that the town I grew up in was full of rich, entitled people, and they hated me for that. Every day I went to school, trying to be tough. I did my best not to let these mongrels get to me, but they were relentless. I felt unwanted, for the first time I understood what my twin went through all of high school; and it was terrible. I went home crying many days. I would tell my mom I was going to quit school and work at a fast-food restaurant. Enduring their harassment was almost unbearable, but I did my best to pull through and complete school. I brought vodka in water bottles so I could ease the stress of my bullies.

When I became a junior, I recognized Brittany, a friend from my high school fashion class. She had a friend named Krista and, for the most part, they kept to themselves. They were sweethearts with backbones. If you tried to mess with them, these women were tough. Thankfully, Brittany and Krista bonded with me and began looking out for me. If not for them, I would have quit cosmetology school and never gone back. They were my only sense of comfort in the most uncomfortable situations. My friends had completed more hours than I had, so I knew I would have to finish my last few months without them. I was distressed. It engulfed me, the fear of having no protection against my enemies. I dreaded the day Brittany and Krista would move on and graduate. I thought this was my biggest dilemma in life, but I soon found out I was horribly mistaken.

I was still dating Stan at the time, and we had a mutual friend named Penny. Her father was a musician, and Penny lived an exciting life, touring and traveling with him. She also had an amazing voice and would often sing for us. When I started beauty school, I kind of left Stan behind. I would go to school in the morning and to work at night, answering phones at a car dealership. He did not have a job or go to school, and Penny was home from touring for a while.

Near my 19th birthday, I began getting tonsil infections. Time after time, they kept coming back. My doctor ordered me to take a week off from school to have them removed. Right before the surgery, Penny started acting oddly. She gave me gifts and offered to buy me things. When I had surgery, Stan began to disappear. He did not come to see me and stopped answering my phone calls. The weekend before I was to return to school, Stan finally called. He told me he and Penny had begun sleeping together, and they were going to Las Vegas for the weekend. I was devastated. I screamed at him. I fell apart. I cried for days. My first love had completely deceived me. I thought I was going to be with Stan forever. I absolutely adored him, and now he did not want me anymore. My heart was truly broken. My mother comforted me and did her best to distract me from being sad. She took me to the movies and shopping as much as possible. She encouraged me to keep moving. That, in time, the pain would go away, and this whole experience would be nothing but a memory.

Penny had a reputation for sleeping around and having unprotected sex with strangers while on tour. Apparently, she and Stan had also picked up a hefty cocaine habit. They were spending more than $150 a day on the drug. I believe that is why Stan did what he did. Blinded by addiction, his actions became selfish. He forgot all about me. He did what any addict would do, he got closer to the source. Penny had money and cocaine. She had everything he wanted, and she wanted him. With all these facts, I decided to get tested for sexually transmitted diseases. I had a gynecologist I had seen for yearly exams, so I went to get tested. At the time of the appointment, the nurse told me everything appeared normal. They took a small biopsy from my cervix for additional testing and would contact me with the results.

The following week on my way home from school, the doctor called and asked me to come in immediately. Something was wrong, and I raced to the office full of rage at Penny and Stan. I had trusted people who were dirty, selfish liars. My poor judgment burdened me with a kind of sickness. I was terrified of what the doctor would say. When I arrived, the doctor and nurse took me into a room. They explained I had contracted human papillomavirus (HPV) from this unfortunate situation. Due to how it had progressed, Stan had probably been with Penny for quite some time and passed the virus on to me. HPV, when untreated can cause cancer, and that is what had happened. I had cervical cancer. I can still remember hearing the nurse say it for the first time: "You have *cervical cancer*."

I was informed we would be scheduling a visit for my first treatment. I had cancer. Stan picked up a cocaine addiction, a slutty girlfriend, and because of his selfish choices, I had *cancer*. I should have listened to the warnings from the health teacher in high school about contracting STDs. Whether he was my boyfriend or not, he was still capable of giving me something; and I really did not think having unprotected sex with him was all that dangerous. I could not have been more wrong, and this situation was the evidence to prove it. I was only 19. In accepting what I had just learned, my legs turned to jell-o and my mind went into a frenzy. Did cancer mean death? Didn't people die from cancer? Did this mean I would not be able to have children? What were they going to do to me? Cut pieces out? Remove my reproductive organs entirely? What would I tell my mother? My siblings?

I could barely walk to my car. It was like I could feel the actual infection begin to weaken my body. I remember having to call my mother and stammer out the words, "Mom? I have cancer." It was horrible. My parents were heartbroken but reminded me that my part in this situation was equal to Stan's. As a teenager, I did not think clearly about things like unprotected sex. I was angry and refused to take any accountability. I was still trying to come to grips with the idea that I had cancer. As a family, we came together for the three treatments I had to undergo.

The first was horrific. My twin accompanied me. The doctor came highly recommended. We went into the room together. Ro sat beside me. We were there for a few hours. The doctor cut out various pieces of my infected cervix. It was excruciating. It felt as if he was cutting out my femininity. My sister was worried and uncomfortable as one would probably expect in such uncertainty. Twins have the ability to read each other's thoughts in a way. From time to time, it was like we knew what each other was thinking without a word spoken. On this day, I felt she was angry, perhaps at Stan. Perhaps she was mad at fate for putting us in this situation. For having to watch as the doctor cut the cancer out of me. Despite her rage, she was sympathetic at the same time. When it was over, I could not wait to get up and get out of there. Upon standing, the pain overwhelmed my whole body. I almost dropped to my knees. I began to cry, unable to explain. My sister did her best to help me to the car. I felt doomed, like God hated me. Like I was being punished for something I did not even know I did.

Once we got into the car, I remembered this day was my first opportunity to vote. I begged my sister to take me to the local church so I could participate. She was cautious and thought it was an unhealthy idea. She argued that I should go home and rest. I continued to plead with her, and she reluctantly agreed.

When we arrived at the polls, the first thing I noticed were the church stairs, about 20 of them. I was devastated. I knew in my condition, climbing these stairs would be impossible. Due to my diagnosis and the treatment I had just endured, I wanted so badly to do something normal. Something as normal as voting. Now this simple request would be denied. My sister looked at me, knowing what I was feeling. So she got out of the car and came around to the passenger door. She opened it, and I looked up at her. She looked scared and unsure. I needed her now more than ever, and for whatever reason, she understood the importance of accomplishing this task. She helped me to my feet, and we walked slowly across the parking lot. When we reached the stairs, I felt helpless. I knew lifting my legs would only aggravate the pain. I felt her put my arm over her neck, and she took a deep breath. My twin carried me up those stairs. Still today, I consider her a hero for the way she was able to be my strength, physically and emotionally. She carried me in, and I walked to my cubicle. On our way out, they gave me a small sticker that read, "I voted." I was as grateful as a small child receiving a gold star. My sister knew how happy the sticker made me, and we proudly placed them on our shirts. She helped me back to the car. The tears continued to flow, partially from the pain, but more so because at that moment I could not have had more gratitude for the very existence of my twin.

She helped me to bed and made sure I had everything I needed. Unfortunately, there would be two more treatments ahead. On April 22, 2008, I received my first negative cancer test result. Since then, I have been so blessed that it has not returned.

Wouldn't it be awesome if this was the happy ending to my story? We are just getting started.

A weird thing about being a 19-year-old cancer patient was that everyone felt sorry for you. No one noticed I was drinking in my room. I still had some liquid Lortab left from my tonsillectomy, and I had a fun time mixing it with alcohol. The opiates did not hook me this time. When the prescription ran out, I stopped taking it. Alcohol was a constant. If I was awake, I was drinking.

At a time when I should have been thankful for my life, I began to fill it up with hatred. Here I was, so young, and I had already withstood cancer and rape, had been cheated on, and had watched a dear friend lay lifeless in a coffin. I took all of these as personal attacks. I was remorseful and angry at the world, and this was only the beginning.

I graduated from cosmetology school and received my license. I began assisting three master stylists at a well-known salon in our local mall. My future looked promising. And then, Mike came into my life. I knew of him from high school, a sort of bad boy with tattoos. My dad had hired him at his auto repair shop as a technician. He was the fuel my addiction would need to take off. He was poison to my self-esteem, and would soon crush my morals. He was nothing short of a beast.

Straight Edge Vs. Heroin Addict

When I met Mike, he claimed to be Straight Edge. Meaning, he did not use any mind-altering substances or toxins. I thought it was pretty cool, so I took the pledge not to drink, smoke or use tobacco. We dated about three years. As time went on, I came to know what kind of guy Mike really was. Within the first few months of dating, a young woman showed up at his mother's apartment claiming to be his girlfriend, and accusing him of cheating. She swore I was some sort of mistress. Mike was a great manipulator. He persuaded me this woman was telling stories and had jealousy issues. He said they had dated in the past, and she refused to let him move on. I believed him. A month or so later, Ro informed me he was putting the moves on her behind my back. He had been sending her text messages that the only reason he was dating me was to get closer to her. I was wrapped around his little finger, so when he told me my own sister was lying, I believed him. He was secretive about his phone. I was never allowed to use it or go through it. My parents hated him. My mother even confronted him about the unwanted advances on my twin. He blew her off. I was so blindly in love, I was unable to see he was destroying me. I was addicted to the idea that we were meant to be together.

After a year or so, he moved in with a coworker and her boyfriend. The couple were known to use drugs, but I was not sure it was true. This condo ended up being the gateway to our relationship's demise. Mike began to drink while I remained sober. Over time there were many women who tried to come forward, saying Mike was cheating. I was in denial and refused to believe them. While I still had a place to live at home, I stayed with Mike a lot. After his drinking increased, the fighting started. He pushed me, slapped me, demanded money and threatened my life. I became so twisted, I would antagonize him, welcoming a fight. I would insult him to the point that he would hit me. We got in fistfights almost every night. I was questioned at work for coming in with bruises, exhausted. My manager was concerned with my well-being and work performance. My relationship was beginning to negatively affect every aspect of my life. It continued for a while. Then I turned 21.

Finally able to drink legally opened the floodgates for uninhibited drinking. I figured if he could drink, so could I. At first I felt childish for joining Mike in using any sort of substance after pledging Straight Edge for over a year. I enjoyed the escape and thought maybe it would help me cope with my relationship. So I sought bars that welcomed me. First, I was a regular on Friday and Saturday. Then, I added Sunday. Soon Thursday, until I was a regular every night. I knew deep down Mike was cheating, but being drunk kept me from caring about it. I knew the second I walked in the door he was going to fight with me, and a punch in the face was easier to absorb with alcohol in my system. I honestly felt trapped. I did love him, but this relationship had spiraled out of control and, sooner rather than later, we would crash and burn.

His drinking career became his main focus, although his behavior was not that of someone who drank. He was often too tired to stay awake, or extremely angry for no reason. He was thin to begin with, but now his bones were in clear sight; and he looked as if he suffered from starvation. One night as he lay passed out in bed, I began to look for evidence of something more than alcohol. Quietly I went on a scavenger hunt for answers. In a desk drawer, I found a syringe. My stomach dropped. I checked his arms, but they were unblemished. How could this be? Maybe the needle was not his. Then I noticed he was wearing socks. This was odd. I could not recall a single time he had slept with his socks on. I carefully removed one and was cautious not to wake him. There it was, the truth between each one of his toes. Blatant track marks. He was using heroin.

For some reason, I failed to see a way out. If I left Mike, I would be alone. I hated being alone. Part of it was fear. I was uncomfortable with the person I was. It was easier to date someone who captured my attention, rather than allowing myself to focus on my shortcomings. Then one night at the bar, I was greeted by a group of young women. They told me how they *all* had been victims of Mike's games. He had invited them into the condo and had sex with them in the bed I slept in every night. They had all slept with him and, when asked about our pictures on the wall, he told them I was his sister. I was sick to my stomach. I threw up in the dive bar bathroom for over an hour. When I finally washed my mouth out, I caught myself in the foggy, dirty mirror. Who had I become? I was an unsightly, miserable drunk. I knew what I had to do. I drove to our condo. I barged in, grabbed my belongings, yelled: "*Fuck you!*" and I left. I had hoped I would never see Mike again.

My parents were relieved to have me home, but my drinking escalated. I was having Kahlua in my morning coffee and shots of whiskey before bed. I kept bottles in my car for midday pick-me-ups. My life revolved around the drink. I depended on it. Without it, I was unable to deny the things I mostly hated about myself were my fault. I was able to hide behind the drink to avoid reality. I loved the way it made me dizzy. In cases where I was too dizzy to walk, I would wonder if I was dreaming or awake. That was my favorite feeling produced by substances. I did not have to be accountable or present because I was not even sure what had really happened or what I had imagined. Clear and rational thoughts were a thing of the past, and I was convinced I did everything better while drunk. Driving, sleeping, laundry−everything−was much more entertaining when I stumbled around and sloppily got through the day.

My favorite bar was a shithole called Akery's Tavern, an entry to a trailer park down the way from my house. There was a problem with the sewage, and it always smelled terrible. Tuesday was $1 beer nights and $3 pitchers. They did not serve hard alcohol, but they did not mind if you brought your own if you drank it on the patio. We spent most of our time on the patio with rotting lawn furniture and vomit stains in the cracked cement. I had met some new friends at the bar who drank as much as I did. The one woman with whom I mostly interacted was Jen.

She was in her early 30s, and I knew her younger brother. After getting to know her, she told me she was looking for an apartment and a roommate. She said it would be a great idea for us to be friends and then persuaded me to move in with her. My parents hated this plan and found it awkward that Jen could not find someone her own age to live with. After a month or so of looking, we found the perfect place in Sherman Oaks. Little did I know, this apartment would be the trailhead to my opiate addiction path, and Jen would be my guide.

Moving Into Insanity

Jen and I found a spacey apartment on Dickens Street. It was beautiful, and the complex was quiet. My parents had urged me to stay home. They did not believe I was ready to be out on my own yet, but I craved freedom. I knew that over time my parents would grow weary of my alcohol use, so it would be better to move into a place where I could drink whenever I wanted. I remember packing my things and looking at my empty room. I felt an awful feeling in my stomach like I was making the wrong decision. My parents' house was beautiful and most definitely my home. I was hopeful that my apartment would be my new home and that I would feel comfortable there. Perhaps I actually thought it possible for this situation to work out, but Jen gave me an uneasy feeling. It was as if, she liked me, but she really didn't. She was impatient with me, rolling her eyes and walking away from conversations. I shrugged it off and assumed it to be the age difference, that she was more of an adult than I was. My immaturity seemed to test her patience. If ever I felt uncomfortable, I took a drink. Everything in my day started revolving around alcohol.

In the beginning, I preferred vodka. Vodka and cranberry juice was my favorite, three or four a night. Jen and I found bars we went to regularly. If we did not go to the bar, we would polish off a bottle of wine at home. After a while, the hangovers began to be debilitating. People at work noticed I was having trouble. Sometimes, I would get sick in the mornings and throw up, but I found comfort in knowing I could chase vomiting sessions with more booze. I did not think much of it. As a matter of fact, I assumed that I had a sensitive stomach. I failed to see the drunk I had become and refused to blame anything on the drink.

I soon began to run out of money. The rent and my drinking habit were about the same in cost. I would skip eating most nights, as long as I was able to pick up a $5 bottle of wine on the way home. Daily tips paid for gas to and from work. My eating habits were unhealthy from back when I had starved myself after the summer camp rape. It was another form of self-mutilation. I would sometimes go for three or four days without food. Starving yourself was like being high; when your body started to shut down, you became delusional. I would eat when the fatigue would be disabling. I would get to the point where I should have been hospitalized and deal with the trauma as some sort of high, then eat just enough to keep myself alert and alive.

Three or four months into living in our apartment, we went out to our local bar for a Wednesday night drink. Jen seemed unusually happy this night. She had been to the dentist earlier that afternoon. I was curious because I was not particularly happy after a visit to the dentist. I asked how it went, and she told me of her root canal and laughing gas. Also, that she had been sent home with some medications.

Later in the evening, about three drinks down, she pulled out a bottle of pills. Our fourth drinks arrived, and she said, "Here, take this. With your next one."

I was worried, considering I did not have a toothache. I think she saw the concern in my face, so she assured me it would be fun. Vicodin.

That is what she had given me. Twenty minutes later, I felt incredible. Inside and out, I was at peace. Everything was wonderful. Like the Cheshire Cat from *Alice's Adventures in Wonderland*. Without a care in the world. Nothing mattered. The world and everything in it were fantastic. My relaxed body tingled. I felt as light as a feather, like I could fly. Now I understood why Jen was so happy. Frankly, I liked her this way. She was much less uptight.

The next day, I woke up with a hangover much worse than any I had ever experienced. I felt weak and tired. It was difficult to move about the apartment or to come up with a clear thought. Jen had already gone to work. I thought of taking a shot, or having a glass of wine, like I normally would. It did not seem as exciting that day. I wanted another pill. I tried to erase the thought. I mean, come on; that would be stealing.

We shared the master bathroom, and I went to get ready to shower. I opened the cabinet for the toothpaste, and there it was. Her bottle of pills. Left all alone. My stomach sank. What was I doing? What was so great about these pills that I needed to contemplate stealing? I was not a thief! I took the bottle, but just to see how many were left. There were a lot. Perhaps 30 or more. Then the rationalizations. Surely, Jen would not notice one missing pill. Besides, I really was not feeling well. Perhaps it would help ease my headache.

After the shower, I felt much better as I did the night before. At work, I was friendly and diligent. My boss seemed pleased with my attitude. I had a wonderful shift and headed home. I arrived home early, before Jen. I did not pick up any alcohol that day. I thought I would take a quick nap before making dinner.

I woke up three hours later. Jen would be home any minute. My head was thumping. I felt sick to my stomach. My whole body ached. I was dizzy. Something felt seriously wrong. I began to panic. Maybe I had contracted some sort of flulike virus? Maybe another pill would help? Yes, that would make me feel better. So I dragged my feet into the bathroom, stole a pill and waited to feel better. Nothing happened. It did not work. I wondered if I needed a drink. The night before, I had done both; perhaps that was what I was lacking. So I grabbed my coat and headed for the liquor store. I grabbed a bottle of white wine and some chocolate, then scooted back home. As I walked I decided to open the bottle and take a quick drink.

When I arrived home, I realized a quick drink meant half the bottle. Jen was waiting in the kitchen.

"Hey, can I ask you something?"

"Sure," I said.

"My bottle of Vicodin on the bathroom counter. You take any?"

Fuck. Busted. I was so stupid. I forgot to put the bottle away! What would I say? What would she say? I began to feel nauseous.

"Um, oh yeah, sorry about that. I had a bad headache, and the Advil wasn't helping." I stuttered out this sorry excuse, anticipating her response.

"No worries. Buy me a drink or somethin' later. You feeling better?" she asked.

There it was. The door to addiction and all its secrets had been opened. If I wanted more pills, they could be traded for booze. What I had done was acceptable. I could not respond to Jen because I ran to the bathroom to vomit the small amount of chocolate and wine I had consumed all too quickly.

What I did not know is, by then I was a serious alcoholic. I had been for some time. By skipping my morning dose of alcohol, I had started to detox from it. This was where my sickness was coming from. The opiates were much stronger than the usual downer, so I had escalated my addiction. I was sick from the lack of alcohol and tried to fix it with opiates. By the time I had bought the wine, I had consumed too many opiates, and my body was overwhelmed.

I went to bed early that night. I was convinced I had gotten food poisoning or the flu, denying that substances had any negative effect on me. I ended up taking most of the Vicodin, but Jen had two refills. As long as I brought home booze, she did not mind sharing. We kept up this routine for months.

On a Saturday night in the summer, we went to our favorite dive bar, The Bottom of the Barrel. They had karaoke on the weekends, and we sipped our drinks while watching the locals belt out their songs. This night, there were two studs at the bar. I told her I thought the one with the dark hair was cute. I talked to him for a while. He seemed nice. I never had much self-esteem, so any attention made me feel good about myself. Jen and I brought home strangers and slept with them all the time. It was part of our drunken addict's lives. No one wanted to date us when they learned how much we drank and how likely it was that we used opiates. One night stands were the best relationships we could get.

I got up to go to the bathroom. When I came back, Jen was making out with the guy I had been talking to. I was so angry at her for being selfish enough to discard my feelings. I insisted that we leave immediately. She disagreed and wanted to stay with the guy. Normally, we walked to and from the bars, which were only a couple of blocks away. The buddy system had kept us safe so far, but I was so annoyed I decided to walk home alone.

I was dressed too provocatively to be walking alone in the cold night air. A small dress, no coat. High-heeled boots added to the freezing balancing act of drunkenness and dishevelment. I was nearing my street when a car full of men pulled up alongside, stopping traffic in their lane. The passengers asked where I was going. I ignored them, shaking more than ever. They were blowing kisses and licking their lips. A car behind them honked. They demanded I get in. I lost my breath, paralyzed in terror. They were going to hurt me. Kidnap me. Have their way with me. I started to cry. More honking. I started to run the other way. They copied my move, turning their car around.

"We're gonna rape you, you little bitch!" they threatened as the tires squealed. I had to get away fast. A few steps ahead appeared to be safety, a large shrub. I darted to it and jumped inside, directly into the center. My arms and legs were bleeding from the branches. The car circled a few times looking for me, some of the men got out and began searching for me on foot. Through the branches I saw a knife in one of their hands, I knew I was in serious danger.

I hid in that bush for 10 hours, and I dared not move or make a sound. I started to see people walking by in the early hours of the morning. I climbed out, only injuring myself more. I was across the street from my apartment, and it had not even registered. I ran inside and began to bawl. I was so grateful to escape. Jen came into the living room and questioned my distress. I told her of the situation, that she had hurt my feelings; so I left the bar. She scolded me, saying I was too immature. She could not help that the boy had liked her and not me. She said my story seemed unlikely, and I was just being dramatic.

I never walked home alone again. I always took a cab, even if I was just a block away. After that, the tension between us grew more and more by the day. I guess the truth was I never considered her a friend. I knew deep down what she was to me: simply an exit strategy. The apartment and Jen were all a part of my plan to explore substances and a life without the rules or consequences I had to obey at my parents' house. The ability to have the freedom of an adult that I had so desperately sought my entire life. That was the itching feeling that drove me to get out of my parents' clutches, and I just knew I would be better off on my own.

One Friday night, Jen was out, and I stayed home. I had swallowed a good amount of pills and drank half a bottle of vodka. I got lost in a movie and started to drift into the daze I craved from being high. Then, I heard a knock on the door and stumbled to answer it. I put my eye to the peephole to view my uninvited visitor. It was Mike. He had been texting earlier, but I had not responded. I opened the door, and he pushed his way in. An eccentric, he was always carrying on about how much he loved me. Now, he was frantically going on about how he needed to find a new place to live and something about being in trouble with the police. He was talking so fast, I could only comprehend bits and pieces of what he was saying. I told him to sit down and try to relax for a moment. Frustrated, I went to my room to get something, but I absent-mindedly nodded off while sitting on the floor. The next thing I knew, I woke up in my bed, next to Mike. It appeared as though we had tried to have sex, but we were both so fucked up, it might have been easier to complete a jigsaw puzzle.

Sobering up, I began to understand some things were wrong. First, this apartment complex had tight security; you could not get in without a key and PIN code. Second, the garage gate only opened by remote programming. Even more chilling was the third oddity. I had never told Mike where the apartment was. I assumed my coworker, his roommate, could have volunteered this information. But even then, how in the hell did he end up at my front door? I felt threatened and woke him up.

"How'd you find me?" I demanded loudly.

Mike was too high to respond. I then went to get another pill for myself. My stash was gone. He came uninvited and robbed me of my stash. I went into a fit of rage and pulled a knife from the kitchen. He had used me for the last time. I threw his skinny body off the bed, climbed on top of him and put the knife tightly to his throat, opening the skin just a tad.

"You'll never come back here. No matter what, at all costs, you'll leave me alone. I'm dead to you, understand? If ever you track me down again, I'll slit your fuckin' throat. I swear to God, I'll fuckin' gut you. Don't ever come near me, ever again. Now, get the fuck out!"

He had worked me into a murderous lather, and I meant every word. Mike threw me off him and ran out of the apartment. The door swayed and remained open. I shut and locked it. I never saw or heard from him again. If a man ever made me feel threatened, I got extreme. After being attacked, in questionable situations, I turned into a violent psychopath.

Things began to go south at the salon. I had been promoted from an assistant to a stylist. I had my own station and was busy, steadily building a clientele. However, my paychecks were no good. The salon had its own struggles, mostly because a majority of the stylists were addicts like me, and most of us used at work. The salon's reputation began to get tarnished.

Clients stopped coming back, and the paychecks were bouncing.

Jen and I ended up breaking our lease because I was unable to pay my half of the rent. Little did Jen know, I was spending the little money I had on pills from the women at the salon. Depending on who had what, I was always using something. I started to catch onto their game. They would go to the emergency room, or urgent care, and complain of pain or anxiety. Then, they would get prescriptions for all kinds of things: Vicodin, Norco, Valium, Xanax, whatever they had not used recently. This way, it would not bring any attention to them.

There is sort of a junkie code that needs to be learned. It is possible prescriptions will be investigated, especially if it is for the same medication but from different facilities. Pharmacy workers look for any sign that may expose a drug abuser or dealer. As a junkie, you must cover your tracks, not only the needle marks on your arms, but multiple diagnoses for multiple disorders. Thanks to the internet, you can easily find the most common symptoms to display to the doctors who will prescribe the substances you crave.

Drug addicts are excellent manipulators. We lie about anything and everything to keep our addiction fed. We learn what methods do, and do not, work.

If you want to avoid being arrested, or to even look suspicious, you have to do it by the book. It is a well-known truth that it is a felony to be caught with pills without a prescription. Although they pretend it does not happen, once you have been convicted, hospitals put a red tag on your file, identifying you as a drug addict. Once you are red-tagged, getting prescriptions or pain injections is next to impossible unless you find a crooked doctor who will take cash. Many addicts can take an entire bottle, a whole month's supply, in a day. This is why you go to multiple doctors, multiple hospitals and multiple pharmacies. Although it may be hard to believe, there are blueprints to prolong addiction and avoid arrest. The trouble we face as junkies is drug tolerance. It eventually builds and builds so we need more and more pills to keep us functioning. Then, we get sloppy. We start to "fiend" with panicky calls to pharmacies, demanding our prescriptions be filled immediately. We cause a scene in the emergency room when the staff wants a drug test before administering pain meds. The truth is the red tag is inevitable.

Some last for months avoiding it, some for years, but as a junkie, your need for substances will become more and more desperate. It is known among addicts that the red tag is your ticket to heroin. Once you have been tagged, your options of filling that growing opiate addiction are limited.

Diving deeper into my addiction, now homeless and jobless, I did what every kid does when she has failed: I went crying to my mommy. She got me a job as a cashier at one of the car dealerships and agreed I could move home. My youngest brother, Emmet, had already moved into my old room, so I would sleep on the couch until my other brother, Zack, shipped off for the

Navy. Then I could stay in his room. Finally, I felt safe. I felt like this was my chance to get my life back on track. I promised to be professional and succeed at my new job. And, in the beginning, I worked very hard.

A few months later, police asked me to answer some questions about Mike. He had been arrested and convicted of multiple statutory rape charges. He was 27 and some of the girls were as young as 14. I was shocked and agreed to help by reaching out to Mike, asking about his involvement with young teenagers and letting police record phone calls and text messages that would incriminate him.

Jen and I never spoke again. She felt like we lost the apartment because of me. I do not believe she was wrong. She drank as much as I did, and no matter what the truth was, two addicts do not make a home. She craved the drink, which was legal. I craved the drug, which was not. I was living a dangerous life, chasing opiates with alcohol. I did not care about Jen, or the apartment, or anything. The job my mom found for me guaranteed me money. I needed money to get high, and without rent as a factor, I could spend everything I made on substances. In my eyes, I felt like I had succeeded in building my foundation to have my substances readily available without worrying about any ramifications. This was just another way my addiction had manipulated me into thinking it was possible to live a functioning life as a junkie.

Junkie Soul Mate

When I was in elementary school, I met Sam, the most popular and coolest of all the girls. When she invited me to have lunch with her, I felt accomplished. We stayed friends throughout our lives, but lost touch for a while when she moved out of state. She contacted me after I reached out, writing her a letter. I had just moved home and was lacking friends. Sam came back into my life at what seemed the perfect time. She told me of a car accident that had badly injured her knees. She was prescribed Norco. Sam enjoyed going out, drinking and having a good time. We were young, and I had fun with her. Every weekend, we would party. I often came home late and rarely saw my family.

Working for the dealership, I began to lose focus. I was unable to get into my car without a sedative. I would arrive at work by 9 and would be jonesing another dose by 10:30 or so. I would smoke opiates on my lunch break, and by the time work was over, I was suffering alcoholic tremors. My parents and coworkers worried about my condition, and I could not understand why. These were the years of my life in which I was supposed to enjoy myself. Everyone was being too conservative and overly worried. That was what I thought anyway, until I recognized I was wrong.

One night, Sam invited me and my sister to her new boyfriend's house in Hollywood, not the good part of the city. It was in a damaged and scary neighborhood. My sister did not really party, but she wanted to hang out with us. Shortly into our drinking and using, Ro became uncomfortable. She had a mutual friend come to pick her up. Sam and I went outside and mocked them both. We were rude and belligerent. If ever someone questioned our drug and alcohol use, we attacked them. Sam had summoned one of her boyfriend's friends, who she thought I might like. His name was Jim. Shortly after his arrival, we did some more drugs and drank more. I was dancing with Sam in the yard and fell into some dog shit and then went to throw my clothes in the washing machine. I remember Jim following me into the laundry room.

The next morning, I awoke on the couch completely naked. Jim was asleep on the other couch. Embarrassed and afraid, I used my blanket to cover myself and sought privacy. I rushed into the bathroom where I began to vomit. My body was overwhelmed. I had overdone it. My nose was bleeding, and as I looked into the mirror, I saw my ribs jutting out of my skinny, tautly stretched torso. My hip bones were in plain sight. When had I lost so much weight? Sam knocked on the door. I told her I would be out in a minute and continued to clean myself up. I quietly exited the bathroom, found my clothes and went to rush for the door to escape.

Sam stopped me and urged me to stay for breakfast and coffee. I did, and Jim asked me for a ride home. Although every instinct I had was telling me *No*, I agreed to drive him home. The first few minutes of the car ride were quiet. Then he thanked me for a *fun* night. I felt queasy. My worst fears were coming true all over again. What did he mean by *fun*? I had to ask.

He told me of the many, wild sex acts from the night before. I became hostile. I yelled at him and told him he was lying. He looked scared. He assured me I was awake. Well, if I was awake, I believe I would have at least the slightest recollection of what happened. Other than hazy scenes of stumbling about the house, I remembered nothing.

Was this rape? Had I been raped a second time? I dropped him off and drove away. I did not make it far before I had to vomit again. Not because of my consumption, but because this guy took advantage of me, then *thanked* me for it. I had tried to protect myself from this very situation for years and now, I had failed.

When I arrived at home, I ran up to the bathroom and locked myself in. I turned on the shower to muffle my gasps. I undressed and began to examine my body. I had seen it done on the CSI television shows and attempted to come to a conclusion. I was blanketed with bruises. The scariest of all were the silhouetted handprints around my neck, which possibly explained why my throat hurt so badly. In some sadistic sex act, I had been violently choked. Perhaps that explained further why I could not remember anything. I had scratches and bruises on my sides and arms, and my inner thighs told a story of what looked like bruises made by fingerprints prying my legs apart. I had been the object of this man's perverted fantasy, and in his inebriation, he had been brave enough to act it out.

This was the first time in a long time I had really taken a moment to look at myself in the mirror. I hated what I had become. A husk of a girl I once liked. What was left of my morals were hanging on for dear life. Begging me to stop. To save myself before it was too late. I stayed in the shower for an hour or so. I hugged my knees and cried as I tried to wash whatever had happened off of my beaten body. Too ashamed to face my family, I tediously and carefully covered the bruises on my neck and came home even less often until they faded away.

I noticed my mother looked pained. Like she knew of the damage I was doing to myself, but for now, I needed a couple of Norco and some Valium. Just so I could sleep until I knew what to do. "For now" happened to last a couple more months. Then I did away with the thought of what happened and started to smoke Roxys' heavily throughout the day.

I was told my managers at the dealership wanted to let me go, that I had not been doing my work. It was hard to keep a job when nodding off and sneaking away to my car to get high was more important. I missed the cosmetology industry and began looking for jobs to get back into doing hair. This job was corporate, I needed the lax environment of a salon to better hide my drug use.

Zack's departure for the Navy was nearing. He was my confidant, the most valued relationship in my life at the time. He was the only one who had an idea of how bad off I was. I cannot count how many times he came to pick me up or check on me to see if I was safe. Soon I would be losing my best friend and protector to wherever the Navy shipped him.

My parents had a strict rule that I was not allowed to get tattooed while living at home. On this particular day, we were getting ready to go to my brother's farewell dinner. After consuming some opiates and alcohol, I had this wonderful idea. Earlier in the week I had written a poem for Zack. It was about being apart and, that no matter what, when we looked up, we would always see the same sky. That when he looked up to the sky to think of me, I would be looking up to the same sky, thinking of him. What better than to get a tattoo symbolizing my love for him? With hours left before dinner, I called up my beloved tattoo artist and headed for his shop.

The tattoo covered my entire forearm. In driving home from the tattoo shop, I realized that my parents would be infuriated, and in a dumb state of intoxication, I thought I would be able to hide it. I was wrong, and it blew up in my face. At dinner, my mom noticed the tattoo. It ruined the entire event, my mother crying in anger at my selfishness in a restaurant. My dad was furious with my behavior. We went from laughing and appreciating my brother, to arguing. My parents insisted that this was the last straw. It was not the act of getting tattooed, but my arrogant, disrespectful attitude. My brother left for boot camp with his heart weighed down by my inconsideration. I was destroying myself and my family, and now he was leaving. There would be nothing he could do to protect me. He knew I was damning myself to a miserable life. Exhausted by my behavior, he gave up on me that night. He knew I was too far gone and that, even if I begged, he would no longer come to my rescue.

When I got home, my parents told me to pack my things. This was the unconscionable. I had broken the rules one time too many. They were so uninterested in my attitude and behavior, and I had to leave. I could not believe they were actually kicking me out, which is probably why they did.

I ended up at Sam's house. I had nowhere else to go. She was getting high, and it seemed like a good way to relax. We talked for a while, and she convinced me my parents were over-controlling, and I did not need them. I believed her.

After that, I started using more and more. I needed 10 to 20 Norco to make it through the day. I drank a bottle of Jägermeister throughout each day and smoked more potent opiates in between. I started working at a chain salon, and they had me going back and forth between two locations, so I could pay for the room I was renting that I had found on craigslist. I met a girl at the farther location, and she, too, liked to party. Not quite like I did, but she drank enough.

One night, I went to her house as she was having people over. This turned out to be one of the most detrimental nights of my life. At first, it was just me, her and a couple of others. I got drunk fast. I remembered fumbling for my pills. As I crammed them down my throat, I realized I was at a party with a bunch of Nazis. All skinheads. The party had grown at some point. They happened to know my tattoo artist, who was like a big brother to me, but that was all I knew of my fellow partygoers.

That night, I was raped for the third time. Two men. One of the most horrible situations I have ever suffered. I often have post-traumatic flashbacks of what happened. One of them rammed himself down my throat. I was choking, and my mouth was bleeding from the corners. I was positive I would die as I could not breathe at all. This would be my fate. The worst part was I was too high to fight them off. My arms and legs were unable to respond. I could see and hear what they were doing, but my body was lifeless. They absolutely ruined me that night, physically and emotionally. No one at the party tried to help, or stop them. No one cared, perhaps they did not know the men had forced themselves on me. In the morning, I woke up again, unclothed and in the company of one of my attackers. I quickly dressed and ran for my car. When I got there, I fell to my knees. I began shedding tears uncontrollably while trembling. I wanted to scream for help. For any neighbor to come to my rescue and phone the police to arrest these men for what they had done. I was ashamed and wanted to die. I could not live this life anymore. I had had enough. I was disgusted, embarrassed, completely used, and I was entirely alone.

I repeated what I had done after the situation with Jim. I locked myself in the bathroom and hid in the shower. I washed away the attack and carefully concealed any marks that might show evidence of what had happened.

The next day at work, just when I thought things could not get worse, the coworker informed me there was a video of the attack. I do not remember exactly what I said to her, but I threatened to call the police if I got my hands on it. I would press charges against the men.

If you wonder why I never reported any of the rapes, it was simple: A junkie does not walk into a police station to ask for help, not for any reason. I was too afraid police would know I was illegally buying and consuming opiates. My addiction was stronger than my self-worth. I was afraid they might arrest me for illegal drug use more than I cared about bringing my attackers to justice. In reality, they would have asked if I had a drug problem, but they would have hunted for the men who attacked me. Every day I kick myself for not filing charges. It kills me to know they are out there somewhere, looking for their next victim.

A piece of me died there in that party house, and it will never be revived. There are two illusions we perceive as children: That the world is innocent and beautiful, and that we are safe. I experienced the true evils of the world that night. Humans full of hatred without souls, who took whatever they wanted. These beings were capable of robbing innocence from your very bones. They fed on the weak, in the illusion of building strength. They were cowards dressed as tough guys. They were *never* men, and *never* will be. They were nothing but bullies to the fullest extent of the word and are condemned to remain sick and twisted individuals.

I have trouble being intimate with anyone. I am always convinced people are selfish and only want to take something from me. I am a skeptical person. I do not trust anyone without good reason to believe they are trustworthy, and even then, I never fully put my guard down. I covered myself in tattoos and metal, to drive away those drawn superficially to a pretty face and feminine figure. My beauty lies within, and it is heavily protected.

I warn those around me that if the unfortunate situation ever arises where I feel threatened that someone might try, for a fourth time, to take advantage of me; they best restrain me at all costs. For if I feel endangered again, I will tear a man limb from limb with my bare hands. I will fight to the death to protect the microscopic amount of innocence remaining. No longer will I be careless with my body. No longer will predators take advantage of me.

In sobriety, I have become grateful for my choice to protect myself. I do that with everything I have. The greatest of warriors have endured the most pain. The most brutal of beatings, and with those they have gained strength. I am fully aware of what I am capable of doing in an instant when I feel threatened, and I pray no other has to face it. I will be damned if there is a fourth rape, and I will do everything I can to prevent it.

On a side note, I find it relevant to tell you what became of my second attacker, Jim. He got sober, too. We sat in meetings together for more than a year. Jim said he had no recollection of how he knew me, only that I looked familiar. I never had the chance to tell him what happened that night, or what he did to me. Addiction won and took his life some time ago.

While many people around me mourned his death and missed their friend, no one knew how we knew each other or of the night he attacked me. When I was notified of his death, I felt relieved. Indifferent, at best. It was simply over. I would never have to worry about sitting across the room from a man who raped me, choked me and *thanked* me for it, ever again.

In all fairness, Jim was an example of what happens when an addict continues to relapse. I think it made me feel better that he did not remember me, or that night. Part of me found closure that he really was not a serial rapist. He was just a guy who was fucked up and made a terrible decision to act out and use me to get off. Honestly, I do not know that I consider it an intentional, deliberate rape. Other than the evidence that was present, I do not remember anything. I do not think he planned to hurt me. That was the hard truth about using drugs: When you are high, you have no control over what kind of person you are, or what you are capable of.

The House Of Destruction

I often became fidgety in my living situations. I moved back home periodically, when my parents felt sorry for me. I would get kicked out of various places, and I would need a place to stay until I found another room for rent. My parents had a clear limit on the amount of time I was allowed to stay. It was not permanent by any means. Some nights I would fear getting high in the driveway because my parents might notice. Often, I would get into fights with my family because they knew my behavior was suspicious, making my stay only more temporary.

One day in a drug-induced state of confusion, I went to my parents' house convinced my sister had stolen my blow dryer. I went inside yelling and blistering her with accusations. I went into the bathroom and gathered a hair dryer and flatiron, which it turned out did not belong to me at all. I was high and somehow thought these were mine. My sister tried to stop me from taking her things, but I pushed her backwards, almost causing her to tumble down the stairs. Emmet, my youngest brother, was furious. He jammed himself between us, demanding I leave. I tried to push the teen out of my way to continue the skirmish, but he stood his ground. I wanted him out of my way so I dropped everything but the blow dryer and used it as a weapon, beating him in the face. He protected himself and managed to take it from me after a minute or two. He then picked me up kicking and screaming, hoisted me over his shoulder and took me to the front door where he physically threw me outside and demanded I never come back.

During this madness, the person I needed most was my drug dealer. He gave me the doses I needed to keep going. As a junkie, you developed an odd relationship with this person. It was an insane trust in someone you knew was a liar and a thief, but somehow, you believed he would never treat *you* that way, that *you* were special, perhaps more important than the rest. I had run out of places to stay and had found nothing promising in my search for a room to rent. I was sitting with my dealer in his room, chatting while we chased bits of melting heroin down pieces of foil with a straw. He offered to let me stay there for a while.

From the street, this house looked normal. As a matter of fact, it was in a wealthy neighborhood, where the kids played outside. All of the neighbors were friends. It was a gated community, and everyone knew each other. It seemed all the kids carpooled in mommy's new Escalade, and they wore clothes costing enough to feed an orphanage. Money was no object, and you would assume the community to be safe. But this assumption would be wrong. The biggest heroin dealer in town resided at the end of their street. He would think nothing of trading their kid's lunch money, no matter how young, for a bag of dope. Money was money. The house might have had a few clues that went unnoticed: The rotting stucco beneath the window sill from a collection of cigarette butts, the constant traffic of people coming and going, the heavy and dampening feeling you got when walking by a house where you knew someone had died.

Once you walked through the threshold, you could smell the corrosion of souls. You could feel the velvet coffin of death inviting you in to stay. The uncertainty of whether you would make it out alive. The television stayed on and went unnoticed. There were people lying throughout the living room on second hand furniture. They looked dead but were most likely stuck in a temporary, drug-induced coma. The dealer kept them doped up while he emptied their wallets. If they ran out of money or jewelry, he awakened them long enough to throw them out to make room for a new body. I found it odd the neighbors did not notice the zombies stumbling out of this house without direction. It took them time to find their cars, or an idea of where they were. I took it all in. It was as if I was taking in details of the house I had failed to see in the many times I had visited before.

I took my bag upstairs and told myself to make the best of the situation. There were four rooms. I believed his parents stayed there every once in a while, but probably abandoned it after it became too run-down. Perhaps they were drug users too, or maybe he used drugs because his parents deserted him. Whatever the case, there was zero supervision in this house. By legal age, we were adults, but it was clear we made the worst of decisions.

I supposed, as a junkie, one did not examine the bigger picture. Like the fact heroin came from somewhere. That the organization supplying mass quantities of the drug was run by the most ruthless, dangerous human beings walking this earth. And it was a vicious cycle. The dealers, or runners, were the bottom of the food chain. They received their drugs from someone, who then supplied other people, who reported to someone in an even higher chain of command, who had his crew, and so on, and so forth. It all came back to a fierce old man growing and supplying the actual product on some large piece of property in another country. He called all the shots. Maybe that is why they called him a drug lord. To those below him, he acted as if he was God. If anyone put him at risk of discovery, they would be sacrificed to save his drug lord legacy. These people thought nothing of taking a life. They were not like the junkies. We were the demand, they were the supply. This organization was perfectly capable of killing any "risk," and disposing of them. I found it relevant in many cases where people went missing. It happened quickly. Maybe they were unaware of a family member's habit with the drug, or they just happened to get involved with these dangerous people. It was something to consider. Like when Susie went on her morning hike and never returned. Her cocaine habit left her $10,000 in debt, and she told the wrong person to "fuck off."

In my opinion, it was equivalent to jail without the cell. Once you were part of it, you would never get out. If any of the higher-ups thought you were a weak link in their chain, he took your life and replaced you in hours.

What I am about to tell you of this house is nothing short of sickening. I am not proud to have partaken in any of it, and this memory is one of the most chilling.

My room was hardly clean or welcoming, but it had a bed. It was a place to sleep, and in some odd way, I felt safe knowing my dealer's room was next to mine. Upon further inspection, I noticed the bed was stained with urine. Probably cat piss. The stains on the floor were that of poorly cleaned vomit, and with some of the vomit, there was blood. I had to consider someone may have died in this room before becoming vacant. Maybe he or she had OD'd, or maybe this person had been a weak link in the chain. I felt chills run down my spine as I wondered if this was the most perilous situation I had ever faced. Perhaps it was best I left and found a floor, elsewhere, to sleep on. I considered how much more access I would have to substances now. Wasn't it a dream come true? Every junkie lived to be where the heroin came from. I was one of the lucky ones. This bed, this room, was considered a privilege.

I thought the most time anyone spent at their dealer's was probably no more than a few hours. I can assure you that before staying there, I had no idea what ghastly secrets were kept inside.

The first night, there was a bit of a party. Random junkies from all over gathered to get high. This was like no party I had ever been to. There were syringes everywhere. Burnt spoons and lifeless bodies. I felt nauseated watching it.

Some attempted to have sex, but nodded off before they could achieve the act. I overheard one woman talking about her kids. There was a guy in the kitchen fumbling through empty cabinets. He had been in there long enough to realize there was no food, unless he wanted to kill a live rat and eat it. My head pounded, as all of this was too overwhelming. I went up to my room. By the time I curled into my bed, I was quaking.

I heard the cackling of teenagers outside my window, almost a voice outside of my body silently screaming for them to turn around, pleading with them not to come inside. I was curious enough to peek down the stairs at the newest victims. They were high school kids looking for a good time. They had no idea what they had willingly walked into, and by now, it was too late to leave. It was not that any one person kept you from leaving; it was you who kept you from leaving. It compared to driving by the scene of a fatal car accident. Your morals told you to look away and drive by, but you were all too curious. Intrigued by gore and a possible dead body, your eyes widened, excited to take in any hideous image that seduced you to watch.

Although you knew the second you walked inside, this house screamed its warning of destruction; you saw things you had never seen before. Your curiosity was propelling you forward, and you were not going anywhere.

Heroin often made my body physically sick, so after I smoked my early evening dose, in an attempt to escape this terrifying reality, I ran to the bathroom. As I lay between the toilet and the bathtub, I overheard one of my dealer's friends in the next room. There was a girl in there with him. Then, all I could hear were her cries, and she begged him to stop. Being a rape victim myself, I began to weep. I thought I was too high to stop it, and at the same time, I had to help her. I stumbled out of the bathroom in tears and went to the room. I reached for the door and was thrust backwards. It was my dealer. He asked me what I was doing. In tears, I pleaded with him, begging him to help that girl and let her go. He took me back to my room and told me not to worry.

From there, all I could hear was him yelling at his friend. The girl ran out of the house hardly dressed. Despite her frantic state and unfortunate situation, the truth of the matter was hardly in her favor. Now she was a problem. She could tell police everything she saw and identify us all. Including me. They would bust the house, and we would all go to jail.

I nodded off, or maybe passed out to the severity of the situation, but my memory of that night ended there.

Early the next morning, his friend was gone, and he wanted to speak to me. He explained if I continued staying, I was as much a part of this as he was. That law and reason did not exist, and problems were taken care of in other ways. Still high, I agreed. It was empowering in a way. Knowing you were above the law and God-given human rights. That the people, who came into our house, left their lives in our hands. Depending on their cooperation and contribution, we made decisions of what would become of them. These decisions were communicated by exchanged glances. I never once told him I wanted someone to die or disappear; those were not my calls to make. How they would be treated while they stayed, or if we stole from them, or not, was agreed upon in tandem. But who were we kidding? Everyone was robbed. Only when we needed them for something else, such as sex or food, would it prolong the so-called friendship.

The girl did not tell the cops. I never knew what happened to her. But I know his friend, who had caused the girl to beg and cry, was never seen again. When I asked about him, he would ignore me. People often came into this house and completely disappeared. Some of them were found overdosed in random motel rooms. Some of them simply went missing. All I knew is, sometimes late at night, I saw a big, black van show up. The men wore ski masks and did not talk. I never saw what, or possibly who, they took because I was afraid to be seen. As time went on, I knew I had to get out of the place before I also became a body in the back of that van.

I stayed for two months altogether, one of the longest 60-day stretches of my life. I was always afraid if I tried to leave, then I would go missing. I invented the idea that I had to stay there forever, without being told or led to believe this was the case. I convinced myself that I knew too much to get out. I was afraid the men in the van knew my car, or worse, knew my face.

I awoke one day and told him my parents had asked me to come home, and I wanted to rebuild my relationship with my family. A lie just creative enough to get me out of that house. He was genuinely happy for me and wished me luck with my family. So I packed my things and got out of there. I am still not sure where I went after that. I believe I rented a room somewhere. The frightful things that happened in that house still haunt me, especially knowing I used in those rooms alongside bodies that may not have been alive.

If you are curious as to why I did not tell the police about this house, I will do my best to explain: These people were capable of making numerous people disappear in an instant. The people who ran the drug circles have access to plenty of resources. I do not know of anyone who tried to turn them in and lived. I knew and know better. While I was sad for the victims who died as a result of getting involved, they all came in willingly. They wanted to be there and did not care enough about the risk.

I was happy to learn this house was busted by the narcotics unit a couple of years ago. The men who ran the house and the dealer went to prison. While it sounds like a victory, it is not.

These houses are everywhere. The more affluent the community, the less likely they are to be caught. They recruit kids as young as 10 to carry weapons and run drugs for them. There are many drug cartels from diverse countries tied to all these homes and dealers. The only way this will cease is if they run out of clients, which will probably never happen. People like me are obsolete to them. Being sober, I do not remember enough details to tie them to any crimes or deaths. People go in and out of these houses all the time. If you stay too long, they will try to make you part of the business, and if you surrender your life to work for them, they own you forever. There is no crime they cannot get away with. Once you are a part of their world, it is their law and order by which you live. If you are caught, your best option is to be put away in a cell forever. If you are not killed in prison, they will be waiting for you when you get out. Getting caught by police is like stabbing one of them in the eye. It is taken personally. You are trusted to be careful and avoid the law. If you are caught, that mistake is blamed entirely on you for being careless; and clearly, they can never trust you again.

I was able to leave and become a better person. The truth of what I have seen makes the world a different place for me. It is difficult to understand if you have never been a part of it. These dealers and runners are among us everywhere, in every walk of life, in everything we do. They are your bank tellers, your attorneys, your grocery baggers. On the outside, they appear normal. Their homes are tidy. It all adds up. If you become their client, you are their victim. You are their source of income.

If you become a junkie, these people rely on you to keep the money coming in. The ugly truth is, these men and women are needed by addicts, and we will grow in debt to them eventually. You will ask your dealers to front you, not knowing what they are a part of and who they work for. When too much time has passed and they do not receive payment, they will come for blood. While they probably will not take your life, you belong to them, you owe them. You are now forever a victim. The cycle will continue. You will pay off some of the debt and keep using. Your debt will keep adding up, and they will continue to beat you within an inch of your life when your payment lapses. You will sell your belongings and steal to come up with money enough to make right with them. After a month or two, you may have improved your standing sufficiently to buy another hit. At this point, you better pray the drug kills you first. They will only beat you so many times before you disappear.

There is nothing enjoyable about being an addict. There are only so many places you can land if you choose this life. Not one of them is respectable. If you are lucky enough to get sober, you better do anything and everything to keep it, because if you cannot, everything you tried to get away from will be waiting for you. This world of drug abuse only gets darker over time. Junkies are never guaranteed anything.

This part of my story weighs as heavily now as it did when I was living it. I never want to be in a house such as that again. I never want to see and hear again the things I witnessed there. I assure you, if I choose to relapse, that grim future would be all I have to look forward to.

So, while the media paint a fun picture of partying in mansions with the movers and shakers of our time, what I have told you is the ugly truth. This darkness is where you will end up. It is not wealthy parties with beautiful, sexy bodies, or endless supplies of drugs and alcohol. You will sell your soul to these drug lords in order to keep chasing your fix. You will not care whether you live or die. Your life will be an adrenaline-soaked game of Russian roulette, where the cylinder with the bullet offers an unforgiving fate on each spin. You will keep pulling that trigger until the lethal one finally finds you.

I Fought The Law

It seems unreasonable there is so little talk of my involvement with the law. Junkies and jail go hand- in-hand. Breaking the law among junkies is like the process of elimination. It is not that all of us lack education; some of us know how to avoid the police. It is basically desperation that gets our freedom revoked. When we are deep in addiction, and our timing is off, we get sloppy.

My dealer helped me learn what not to do. He told me that while it is easy to get arrested, a charge needs evidence. Lack of evidence reduces your charges or can get you off the hook completely. In so many words, you never want to get caught with junk. Never have anything on you. In traveling from the dealers, you must take every precaution. This means holding off getting high until you have reached your destination.

While I was pretty good at following these rules, it was my alcoholism that got me into trouble. I would steal drinks at bars, start fights and then drive myself home. If you are a junkie, who wants to stay out of jail, you need to avoid attention. Unfortunately, when you are intoxicated, you tend to do stupid shit. While under the influence, rarely do you consider the consequences before you act.

One night when I was in the early stages of my drinking, I had up to 10 cocktails and made my way home. I was pulled over. The cop could see I was tipsy, maybe one or two too many, but he was unaware of my tolerance. I sat on the curb in handcuffs, and as he looked back at me; he let me see the worst thing he could have: I saw his "tell." Everyone has that tell, a look about them showing they are human and weak in emotion. He had sympathy in his eyes.

As an addict, I had to find a way out of jail before I got there. I knew if I ended up in the back of that patrol car, I would be blood tested and in serious trouble. The test would show my blood-alcohol level was way above the legal limit, and that would be evidence to convict me. The ramifications of my actions would cost me the one thing I needed to keep, my means of transportation.

So, I would have to play these cards fucking perfectly. Rarely does someone get out of a DUI. A conviction costs an average of $10,000 in fines, plus a loss of driving privileges. It is super unlikely to get off the hook. Not to mention it is extremely dangerous to drink and drive. I started to cry. He tried to ignore me at first. I continued to pathetically sob to get his attention. First, I had to assume there was a female in his life around my age, possibly one who was in and out of trouble; and somehow I hoped I reminded him of her. Judging by his age, I assumed it was his daughter and prayed I was right. He finally approached, and I blubbered about how I was a daddy's girl. I was pleading that this was the first time I had ever been out drinking, and my dad would be furious. He would hate me, and I would do anything not to disappoint my father. I cried that I was sorry, and if he gave me this one chance, I would never drink and drive again.

Hook, line and sinker. He was hesitant at first, then started to lecture me about the dangers of drinking and driving. I pretended to be stunned and ashamed at his words and only cried more. After a few minutes, he agreed I better never drink and drive, *ever* again. Uncuffing me, he then followed me home to ensure my safety. That was it, the only time I came close to getting caught. I impressed myself with that performance, as it was extremely rare to avoid an arrest such as that.

My dealer, on the other hand, was arrested quite often. He had been a friend of mine since we were kids. I could ask him anything, and he would tell me. He was a genius when it came to the law. He knew the legal definition of every charge and what you could do to avoid it and/or get out of it. Being a huge-time cartel drug dealer, he had to stay educated. Every time he was arrested, the charges were dropped. He was too smart for them. He frustrated the narcotics unit, despite their many hours investigating him.

He would explain a myriad of subjects while we sat and smoked our heroin. He would tell me what must happen for a judge to condemn you to a cell and how everyone has a physical tell, whether it be an officer, a public defender or the district attorney. And if you read it just right, you might be able to play on it until you get your way.

His perception of the world was interesting, and definitely accurate. He talked about religion a lot. How

God wanted us to do the right thing and treat each other with kindness. He would say how we are all a product of government manipulation and that religion kneels to Uncle Sam. Upon my curiosity, he explained further. We are brought up to believe in God, and that the church brings positivity, forgiveness and the proper path to life. Wrong! Church is a scam, like most religious shit. When you go to church, religious leaders ask for a donation. While you bend on your knees at the hand of God and beg his forgiveness, the head of your church counts his money. Then after the service, he sneaks away in his $60,000 Mercedes that your "contribution" helped buy. From there, he drives to his house in his gated community. The government gets paid its sales taxes on these hundreds of thousands of dollars, so everybody wins. His kids attend a private religious school costing $40,000 a year, ensuring they grow up properly immersed in ancient tenets to battle modern thought. This spiritual "role model" may work a regular job during the week to hide that he is fleecing the flock so brazenly.

One might assume heroin junkies do not have much on their minds. But my dealer did, and he piqued my interest. He was the smartest person, truly, that I have ever known. His logic and reasoning were unique, perceptions I had never considered or heard before. Coming from a religious Jewish family, I did not think much of the rabbi or how the temple functioned financially. As a kid I asked my mother how the rabbi paid his bills if he did not have a job. Her response was that his job was being the rabbi. In exploring my dealer's thoughts, things started adding up.

It was almost as if his perceptions and ideas of government and humanity made it acceptable to use drugs and entitled him to be part of the dirty world of addiction. I have to admit it was his advice on avoiding the law that kept me from jail. He often warned if you are associated with idiots who openly talk about hating police, if you are convicted, and if you are constantly in and out of jail; then your time of freedom will be short-lived.

He told me police have access to everything, and our right to privacy is nothing short of a fairytale. The second that police are following, or have a lead on someone, is when they know all of that person's friends and every person they interact with. They can tap your phone, your car, whatever they want. They will get leads to situations and bust you without you having any idea what just happened.

We were high a lot of the time, so I am not sure how much of this is true, but it got me thinking. Enough so, that even at three years' sober, I refuse to enter a place of religious practice, and I will never give them money because the God in whom I believe does not care if I donate to a church.

It is the idea that maybe all of us junkies are lost. Perhaps we live in a world where everyone else is oblivious to the everyday lies we are told. And in knowing we are being lied to, we act out. I cannot stand the thought that some preacher gets to have endless amounts of money for condemning us to a hell that man created.

If we are some druggie; a stealing, lying piece of shit, at least we have the drugs to explain our actions. What about the rest of society who demands our money without reason? The government works against us, demanding we "prove" our income and give them a percentage for allowing us to be "free?" Perhaps it seems frivolous that one might rant about something such as this, but I have a point. I fought against the law with knowledge, and that kept me out of jail. Right or wrong did not matter because it worked. Maybe having the smartest drug dealer in the world, and listening to his rants and ideas are what kept me free. The fact is, every piece of advice he gave me worked, proving he was not completely wrong.

I have met many people in recovery, angry at the world for what it is hiding. Perhaps it motivates their drug use. Maybe it gets them going on these crazy thoughts. It is the few and far between who avoid jail. You can call it luck, but I prefer to label it education.

However, I think I have been punished for the revolting things I have done, which is what brings this book alive. Whether you sit in a cell, or are raped and left for dead, it makes no difference. You will pay a price for choosing a junkie's life. You can count on that. There is no such thing as a successful addict. For some, it takes longer than others to discover this. With addiction, it is guaranteed that you will destroy every aspect of a life you know, and trade it for a sorry excuse to be alive.

Fucking Everything Up

One of the rooms for rent I found was with a friend of a friend. She was known to be an avid partier, so I hoped I would stay here for a while. She had another roommate, an older man. He fancied the party life as well. I quickly discovered they did not party as I did and ended up having to do my best to hide my heroin addiction. They drank a lot, maybe they even did cocaine every once in a while, but it was clear that substances were not a constant for either of them.

Maturity was something they lacked. Everyone was frequently picking at each other. Yelling became our way of communicating. They were among the most judgmental people I had ever met. Not that I was an outstanding human being, but all they did was constantly put down everyone around them. And if they were not together, then they would talk shit about each other. The girl, Allie, was a spoiled brat. Her mom gave her the house after she had graduated from high school. She was often throwing temper tantrums. Talking to her was about as constructive as trying to communicate with a drunken ape. It was sad because, despite her being smart, she was a lazy thinker and a negative person.

The male roommate was surprisingly older than us, almost 60. It was scary because he looked and acted like he was our age. He was a bodybuilder and stayed in good health. Looking back on it, it seems odd he would surround himself with people so much younger.

He did not hang around for sexual reasons because he was gay, but I suppose the whole situation was a bit quirky.

For the most part, I locked myself in my room. I had booze bottles everywhere. I hid my tin foil under the bed and had a stash of small jewelry boxes hiding my drugs. When I first moved in, we all went out to the bars together. The thing about being a junkie is you think you are hiding your addiction much better than you are in reality. I would often pop pills from my purse or grind them between my teeth. After a while, they started asking what pills I was taking. I told them that I had headaches, or toothaches, whatever excuse I could come up with, to get them to leave me alone. The environment became hostile due to the fact they knew I was a drug addict who would not admit it. They judged the shit out of me and would yell things about me when they were drunk and thought I was sleeping. Allie and her friends would throw bottles at my door and yell that I was a junkie piece of shit. I stayed locked away in my room, dreading that I might soon be homeless again. I would do my best to befriend Allie every so often to avoid being kicked out.

I had a guy who was in and out of my life. His name was Zeek. We had met years before when I worked at the dealership for the first time in beauty school. He was a troublemaker who loved to break the rules. He was the kind of guy who brought the party to work and would piss off his coworkers on a daily basis. In the beginning, I had feelings for him, and then it just became convenient. When I would spend the night at his house, there was evidence of other girls everywhere. From forgotten lipstick in the bathroom, to jewelry and bobby pins in random places. I became used to it, knowing we did not have anything more than a physical connection that we sought when lonely. Zeek knew I was toxic, but he did not care. He had a drug problem of his own. His body hungered for cocaine, and he knew I could not live without opiates and booze. We did not talk to each other about using. When we saw each other, we had the same look in our eyes: the look of embarrassment. We knew that what we were doing was fucked up. In order for us to interact, we both got extremely high beforehand. This way, we could avoid emotion and not feel badly about our actions. I cannot speak for Zeek, but I believe we felt the same way. We have a relationship with anyone. In the hopes of making the painful loneliness disappear for a night at a time, we would reach out when we were desperate. We would make small talk, have sex, and then go our separate ways. I know, for me, I needed to do it. He was just as addictive as the heroin. I would leave his house, telling myself each time this was the last time, that I would never come again to see him. Sooner, rather than later, I would need another hit of human connection. Even if it was two loaded lost idiots sleeping together to ease a little pain for an hour.

In reality, I was attached to him. I wanted to be his "most important." I knew he was sleeping with other women, but I wanted to believe he enjoyed being with me the most. Not for the sex, but because somewhere in there, he had actual feelings for me. I wanted so badly to be more important than I was. Zeek did not give a flying fuck about anyone. Women were disposable, and he loved that we always wanted more. But denial is an addict's accomplice. One night I entered his room and saw something new. A girl had left a note in lipstick on his mirror. She signed her name with a heart. I knew he was sleeping around, but I continued to insanely think I was the only one. As I left his house, I decided it really would be for the last time. I went for a week or so without talking to him. Honestly, I did not want to. The lipstick note on the mirror left me feeling betrayed and angry in some unexplainable logic coming from an addict's irrational mind. I felt like he cheated on me, although it was never a secret he was a slut.

A few weeks later, I began to get sick. Violently sick. Not like any "kick" or hangover I had before. One of the women at work suggested a pregnancy test. I thought it was a dumb idea. Due to my experience with cancer, getting pregnant would be a challenge. The doctor warned it would require hormones, scarring treatments and being careful during the entire pregnancy. That when I decided to conceive, it would be a challenge and, even then, there were no guarantees I would be able to carry a pregnancy full term. A week later, I remained ill. No matter what I took, I could not get rid of whatever was keeping me sick.

Frightened, I relented and took the pregnancy test, although, deep down inside, I already knew the test result. It was positive. I hoped maybe it was faulty, so I took another one, then another. Then a boxful. I took a total of 10 over the course of a few hours. Nine of them were positive. I sat on the floor of the tiny bathroom and broke down. What the hell was I going to do now? I figured I could not tell Zeek. We were not even dating, and what would become of this poor, innocent child? This mistake. My whole life was a mistake at this point. This was the moment in my addiction which made it clear I was a failure. My life in its entirety was worthless, and I was an irresponsible, foul excuse of a person. So, I did what I did best, but this time it was not to get high. I got all of my drugs, all of my pills, all of the heroin and all of the booze. I laid them throughout the bathroom, and I ingested them all. Some may assume suicide is a selfish act, but for me it was something else. I did not want to die because my life was a burden. I no longer deserved to live. In my mind, everyone would be better off without me. This baby deserved a better mother than I could ever be. It was innocent, and I was nothing but a criminal. Every moment, I continued to be pregnant, to be alive, I was putting my baby in danger.

If I went for an abortion, maybe they would know I was using and call the police. At this point, everyone hated me. My own family could not stand the sight of me. It would be better for everyone if we both died there in that bathroom. Not one person would be surprised if they were informed that I OD'd. Perhaps the pregnancy would surprise them, but it would be for the best.

I was never afraid of death. I figured we would meet sooner than later. After all, living was not part of my plan. I would do drugs for a few years. And when it was not fun anymore, I would burn out. For a long time, that was the only life plan I had. I guess it seemed as though death found me sooner than I had thought and in a worse predicament. I never wasted time on the thought of heaven or hell. Whether a sinner, or not, I did not matter. I was a nobody. I was a desiccated excuse of a human being. There would be no afterlife for me. Even God would do away with me and end me all together. I knew I was entirely useless.

I decided to do something I had not done since I was a kid; I prayed as I waited to die. Even in the earliest stages of pregnancy, you knew your baby is there. I felt it, and it was a love so great it could not be put into words. A tiny piece of you being re-created, it depended on you entirely for life. Even when it was as tiny as a tadpole, you knew it loved you. It was an overwhelming feeling of love in its most incredible form. Although it seemed unlikely that a drugged-up waste of a woman could love anything, I loved my baby with everything I had. Enough so that I would do whatever I had to ensure its safety, and the most dangerous thing for my baby was me. So, I explained to God that I knew I was unworthy, but could he grant me one request and take my baby back? I begged him to give it to a better mother who could give it a life it deserved. Part of me wanted to get better, to be better and to keep this child. I knew well enough that it was not an option. I could not stay clean. It seemed I could not do anything right. Everyone's pain and suffering was because of me, and now an innocent, unborn child had to die because I was a weak coward.

After ingesting my poison, I waited for the reaper. I closed my eyes in comfort, knowing I had made the right decision. I wanted to die more than anything, for if this baby could not live, then neither should I. Unfortunately, I woke up the next morning. I was covered in bloody vomit. I had fallen asleep sitting up. I could not even kill myself correctly! I sat in the shower for hours. I could not face myself or the world, and now I was out of drugs. So I did what every junkie is good at; I went to my dealer. We sat and smoked some pills. He asked me if everything was OK. I told him everything. Given our history, I felt comfortable telling him of my secret baby and my failed suicide attempt.

As always, he examined it, and his perception put a different spin on it. He told me this baby was a gift, not a mistake; that when it was born, my life would change. And I would get sober and live to provide for my child. It was an opportunity I had not considered, and I believed him. He invited the idea of fate into my life, and I took it.

I called Zeek to tell him about the baby and my newfound decision to keep it. As expected, he was not happy. He drove out to my house, but the conversation got us nowhere. He yelled at me and told me the very idea was repugnant. I told him all he needed to know was that he would be the genetic father of a child. Other than that, I did not need him. Not for money, support, anything. He was furious. I told him I had a doctor's appointment the following week, and I would keep him informed. But he was not welcome to come. Zeek did not know that during our sporadic involvement, while we were sleeping together, I was not involved with anyone else. Whether he liked it or not, this baby was his.

That weekend, we all went out to the bar. Only one of my friends knew of my pregnancy; and as much as it shames me to admit this, I did what I loved doing. I drank and got high. I did some cocaine in the bathroom and had about 10 drinks. I went to sit outside and tried to secretly do a "bump" out of my purse. Just as I held my pinky nail to my nose, I looked up, and there was Zeek. He was outraged. He screamed that I was pregnant; how could I get loaded? I never have gone back to that bar. Not even sober. It was a white trash brawl, and I was the fucking center of the show.

A lot of people lost respect for me that night, whatever tiny bit of it was left anyway. When I got home, I went back to my bathroom hideaway. I hated the reflection in the mirror. A skinny junkie wasting away with a baby in her belly. I wanted to try suicide again but stopped myself. Maybe God was talking to me. I had nothing in this world, and he gave me a child. Or was this the result of sleeping with some arrogant asshole who just wanted a piece of ass? Either way this baby was mine, and if I wanted to have any shot at keeping it, I would have to get clean.

I probably made it a day without pills. I always drank; it was the only constant of my addiction. I wanted to get clean, but I wanted to get high more. The added fact I was pregnant made me feel extra sorry for myself. I figured I would just do just a few pills, drink a couple shots a day, but no heroin.

When the doctor did the ultrasound, there was no baby. He said there was evidence of a miscarriage. He asked if I remembered any heavy bleeding or pain. After the suicide attempt, there was some bleeding. As for pain, that is why I took opiates. I probably would not have known. I was truly crushed. I really wanted to keep my baby, but I knew it was not right for me. I never wanted to hurt my baby, but I was not capable of committing to the pregnancy. The decision I had trouble making had been made for me. I got in the car to go to work, and I continued on about my day. I told Zeek, and he was relieved to hear the news. That night I had to face the big question: Now semi-sober, would I continue detoxing or go back to getting loaded? I got loaded.

It did not matter how much I wanted to get clean, I did not have a chance. I felt horrible because the truth was, my intoxication killed the only chance I had of someone loving or needing me. I wanted that baby. And now, look what I had done. Like every other aspect of my life, I had destroyed it.

I was kicked out of Allie's house and found a room for rent from a lady who worked at the salon. I did not say goodbye to Allie and the bodybuilder; I just moved out. My dad and brother came to help me. They did not talk much. I figured this would be a good start, maybe

I could dumb down the drug use and act like a normal woman in her early 20s.

Soon after I found my new place, Sam got pregnant. I was angry at first. Sam did not care about having a sober pregnancy. She drank and used every time I saw her. I worried for the life of that unborn baby. Sam's boyfriend was a good guy. He had a beer every once in a while, but that was it. She hid her drug use and bar hopping from him well. While I was mad at Sam for being able to keep a baby when I could not, I still needed her. Getting high alone was depressing. Sam kept the party going, pregnant or not.

I started to get lonely, so I created an online dating account. I met this guy who seemed promising. His name was Jack, and he would be the end of me. I did not know it then, but he would be the bottom of the hole I had dug myself into. When we met, Jack told me he was two years' sober. What a pussy, I thought. So I persuaded him to relapse. I moved him into my room, although my landlord did not approve.

My landlord was mentally ill. She often tried to commit suicide, and not like a subtle pill overdose. She drove her truck off of a canyon. She had two kids at home, but she seemed unable to handle her life. We started to trade Norco for Valium, and that ensured I could stay for a while longer.

Jack was a troublemaker and a thief. He would leave for work every morning, but lied about having a job. He would just drive to his dealer's house and get loaded all day. Then, he would steal from somewhere or someone, and go to the pawn shop to get money. I did not care what he was doing as long as he had money and drugs. It was a modern-day Sid and Nancy sob story. Our relationship revolved around getting loaded, and we did, all the time. Sometimes, he would not come home at all. I did not care. As long as I was high, he could be wherever he wanted.

One night at 3 a.m., my phone rang. The caller ID read that it was Jack. I answered, but to my surprise the voice on the other side of the phone was the sheriff. He had picked Jack up on a heroin binge and found some of my belongings. Jack had stolen my checkbook and debit card, cleaning out all my accounts while racking up more than $3,000 in overdrafts. My own boyfriend robbed me, and I was pretty upset. The only thing I did well was work. I had a job and always showed up. Now all my money was gone, and he did not even share his heroin with me!

During his stay at the county jail, I learned of other girls Jack had attempted to hook up with. This guy was a liar, cheater, thief and just all-around toxic. Part of me guessed I could not find a man any better than Jack. So I did what I needed to keep him in my life, despite what he had done to me.

When he got out, I went to see him at his mother's house. He looked good, much better than he had before. He told me he was leaving for drug rehabilitation in the morning. I stayed the night and saw him off. He was not allowed visitors for two weeks, so I followed in his footsteps on a heroin binge, too. I never "slammed" it with a syringe because of my fear of needles. So I sat there all day, smoking with my tin foil, lighter and dope. What used to be euphoria was now just a dull numbness. I would catch myself grinding my teeth as I nodded off from reality. I was often shaking and unusually cold at all times. The opiates put me in a trancelike state where nothing mattered. I was like some ghost floating about the world. I had no feeling, no emotion. I was unable to connect with others. I was lost in this state of mind where the mind barely functioned.

These two weeks were probably the heaviest part of my addiction. I did more dope than ever. I felt like Jack had passed me up. He was going to get sober and be a better person. What a jackass! How could he leave me to get high all alone, while he "bettered" his life? He was the kind of person I hated. Maybe all junkies hated those who made it out of addiction. Substances gave you the idea you just could not do it; and worse, it was not cool to get clean. Drugs were dangerous, and only cowards walked away from substances. Not me, I enjoyed it; I was not afraid of anything.

Fourteen days later, the day finally came to visit Jack. I awoke early, showered and got ready to see my estranged boyfriend. Without my morning dose, I started kicking. For the first time ever, I was out of drugs and money. I panicked; my landlord was not home, so I could not ask her for anything. Then it hit me. Rehab is for junkies. Surely, someone there would have drugs, making my discomfort only temporary.

This was one of the craziest day of my life. In some part of my irrational thinking, I came across the idea that I had stashed drugs underneath the bathroom floor.

I pulled up the laminate floor, but there was nothing there; and now I had ruined the bathroom. I went to the garage to look for something to fix the floor and found a decent-sized bottle of glue. I glued the laminate floor back down and went on my way to Santa Barbara to visit Jack and score some dope.

When I got there, to my surprise, Jack looked great. He was handsome and smart. He was a totally different person, I wondered what magic pills they had given him. He said he had been sober for almost a month, combined with his sober jail time. His wit and sanity came as a result of not being loaded. All of the patients and staff were peculiar. They were obscenely happy and thankful to be alive. It was a summer camp for adults; adults who did massive amounts of drugs. They painted pictures and talked about their feelings. They were all fucking ridiculous. I thought this must be some kind of real-life funny farm. Maybe the staff was drugging everyone with weird happy pills or something. They all overshared their problems with addiction. All they did was talk; they never shut up. But I could not help but feel safe in being there. All of this talk about addiction, and being an addict, got me thinking I was missing something. I could not figure out what it was. For some reason, I wept all the way home. I had an overwhelming feeling of sadness, but assumed maybe I missed Jack more than I thought.

When I opened the door to my room, I saw it in its entirety for the first time: countless bottles, foil, cigarettes and all kinds of paraphernalia. My room was a dark deathtrap. Maybe I was a junkie, too? Maybe I needed rehab? No. I was just having fun. Just like every other 23-year-old. I was not like Jack at all. He was sick, not me. I got some dope I had discovered in my car and went to the bathroom, but for the first time, the foil and dripping heroin were uninviting. I realized the fix I was always chasing would never come. No matter how much heroin or alcohol or pills I took, whatever it was I was looking for; it did not exist. I was running on a track that would never end. I missed my family so much. My beautiful twin sister and my incredible brothers. My parents and their unconditional love. I could not even remember the last time I spoke to any of them. It was my moment of clarity, that at one time I had a life without drugs and alcohol. Despite my claims of enjoying being high, the life I remembered was much more enjoyable.

I went to Sam's, hoping she could shed some light on the situation. She was on her balcony doing heroin. She had a needle in her arm as she looked up at me. She was nine months' pregnant. My heart broke for her baby and her boyfriend, who knew nothing of what she was doing. I left without saying goodbye. I needed an answer, an end to all of this. What was I doing? When did this become my life, and how could I stop it? I had to do something. Anything to end this nightmare. My veins moaned for opiates, and I started to be sick. I needed a fix, and it was the last thing I wanted. I wanted to be stronger than the drugs. So I dropped to my knees and surrendered to a God I did not believe in. I needed help. I had dug myself into a black hole of drugs and deceit. I needed an answer. For a ladder to drop down and give me a way out. I needed anything. For the very first time, anything *but* heroin.

What Have I Done?

I sat in my car for a long time. I felt abandoned. Nowhere to go. No one to talk to. The rehab center put things into a new perspective. The patients had everything: family, support and confidence. Their only *want* seemed to be the desire to be sober. I did not know if I wanted sobriety or not. I had never considered it seriously before. All I knew was this life. Drinking and getting loaded. The thought of giving that up to be some prissy, sober wimp was so boring. Maybe this is what I needed. If I loved this life so much, then why was I sitting in my car bawling my eyes out?

Where would I start? How does someone get help? Surely, I did not want to go about it the way Jack did. I had yet to find myself in trouble with the law, and I did not want to start now. I remembered my old friend from high school, Clair. We used to smoke weed and get drunk together all the time. I heard through the grapevine she was sober. I had not talked to her in years. I did not know if calling her now would be welcome, or warranted. I had nothing to lose. When she answered, I lost my voice. I could not muster up any words, just sobs. She told me to come and pick her up. I was afraid to see her and wondered what she would think of the state I was in. She got into the car. I realized she was pregnant, but she looked happy and healthy. She did not judge me at all, she just hugged me for a moment and told me to trust her. I had a million questions for her, but I felt numb. I was cold and beginning to suffer the misery of withdrawal.

She directed me where to go, and we ended up in front of a small house, next to an elementary school. It was an outpatient rehab center. I was hesitant to go inside, but I trusted Clair knew what I needed better than I did. A man greeted us. He was tall and tattooed. John shook my hand and offered me a seat. Clair walked me in, then left John to do his work as he shut the door to his office. He was kind and tried to make me comfortable, starting with small talk about where I grew up and how I knew Clair. I started to question my decision to be there. I suddenly felt out of place, vulnerable, awkward and uneasy. I told him I really did not need this. I assured him that I was not like the lowlifes who needed rehab. He did not push me; he merely asked me to take him through a day of my drug use. I decided it would not hurt, so I did my best to recount my dependency accurately.

I began to tell him how many pills I consumed, how many bottles I drank, and how much heroin I smoked per 24 hours. By the time we had gotten our numbers together, he assured me I was in the right place. In one day, I consumed an average of 60 Norco, one big bottle of alcohol and a bit of heroin. He estimated the number of pills needed for someone my height and weight to overdose. On pills alone, it would be around 14. Just in Norco, I should have died five times a day. I was tempting death every time I ingested substances of any kind into my body.

These facts were hard to swallow. What had I become? Some junkie piece of shit? A fucking drug addict? He suggested I stay in rehab at least a week. That, if I hated rehab, I could go right back to doing drugs. This seemed to be a good agreement for me, so I agreed. He asked if I had any substance-related items in my car. I said I did not think so, but I was not entirely sure. He went to my car with me to check. I was wrong. There were at least 100 pill bottles. There was a microwave in the trunk with alcohol and foils inside. I could not fathom that my car had become this drug-infested stash on wheels. Maybe I had gotten used to it? It took us some time, but we threw away everything that had anything to do with substances.

My mother had often accused me of sneaking into the house and stealing her lupus medications. I told her she was crazy, and I had never done such a thing. Now as we emptied the car, it was undeniable. Bottle after bottle, her name was on the labels. I was shocked. I had no recollection of stealing any of these. When could this have happened? I wondered how much my mother suffered, not having the medications she needed to stay healthy, and how much pain and damage I had inflicted on her. I was willing to let my mom suffer so I could get high. I was wickedly inhuman, and even more awful, I did not even know it.

I went to my first group session that night. Everyone checked in, said their names and how many days they had been sober. I refused to participate. I just said my name, and that was it. They all said hello and asked why I was there. My attitude sucked. I was pissed and mean to everyone who tried to get to know me. And I did not want anything to do with them. These people were sick. Hopeless addicts, and I did not belong. I was not like them. Didn't anyone consider that I was just having fun? I had a job and a place to live. I was not some worthless, homeless addict, wandering the street and begging for money. *They* had a problem. Not me.

After group, one of the guys came to talk to me. He asked if I was taking anything to help with the detox. I did not understand, because other than feeling a bit clammy, I was fine. He explained when someone gets clean, they often get sick for a few days. Your body lacks the substances it depended on, and it goes into withdrawal. I was afraid of the unknown, of what was going to happen to me. I had kicked before, but not from all substances at the same time. He offered me Suboxone, a prescription drug to help lessen the debilitating, wall-climbing withdrawal pain while helping to ease opiate cravings. I decided to hang on to it, but I was not going to take it unless I actually got sick. I went home and watched a movie, then went to bed.

I woke up about 2:30 a.m. My body was covered in sweat. My head was hammering so badly I thought my eyes were going to explode. I felt death would be an improvement, then I began to vomit. I spent the whole night in the bathroom throwing up, shivering and feeling like I was going to die. I slept for an hour or two at a time. In the morning, I graduated to throwing up blood. I was convulsing uncontrollably. I definitely thought I was going to die. Then, I remembered my new friend and his recommendation. I dumped out my purse and desperately searched for the Suboxone. I took one and felt somewhat better. It did not take away my symptoms completely, but it reduced the intensity.

Jack's mom had called to see how I was doing. She was truly an angel. For the first time, I told her the truth. That I, too, was in rehab, and currently detoxing. She explained Suboxone was to be taken for a few days, so she helped me get more.

That Saturday, I went to my first meeting. Jack's mom came for support as I was afraid of going alone. It was a speaker meeting. The headliner was a beautiful, older woman with an infectious smile. When her turn came, she unabashedly declared, "I'm just your average coke whore!" I related to her instantly, and loved her fearlessness and honesty. I listened to her story, hanging onto her every word. She came to the part when she got clean. She said, "I got sober and never looked back. I've yet to relapse, and I currently have 15 years' sober. I've kept my original date, and I wouldn't have it any other way."

In that moment, I decided to do the same. I did not feel "sober" while on Suboxone, so I do not count those first few weeks into my sobriety. My first date without a drink or drug without a narcotic crutch was March 29, 2012.

My detox was torture. No person would ever want to experience it twice. I detoxed from opiates, benzos (Xanax and Valium) and alcohol at the same time. I did not feel better until almost 90 days' sober.

My family refused to talk to me or support me through rehab. They thought it was just something I was doing for attention, or an attempt to get them to give me money. My mom checked in on me every once in a while, and John called her periodically to report on my progress.

At 90 days, the rehab had a graduation for me. I invited my whole family. They came, which was surprising. We all sat in a family focus group before the graduation. They asked that the parents, or siblings, check in with the group and say how they were feeling also. Ro was in tears the whole time. When John got to her, he asked why she was so upset. She said, "All of this time, I've feared losing my brother because he's in the military, and it's dangerous. Until tonight, I didn't realize how close I was to burying my twin sister. I hope she stays sober because I don't want to fear losing her every day."

My heart shattered. Hearing that was one of the most painful and beautiful aches I have ever felt. I felt accountable for the first time. I was causing my family heartbreak and worry. I felt selfish and inconsiderate. I decided I did not want my family to hurt because of me ever again. That my mother should never spend another night crying and wondering what had become of her daughter. That my siblings would no longer drop their heads in shame when asked about me. I vowed at that very moment to *never* again be the person who walked into that rehab 90 days earlier.

I did not know at the time what sobriety would be like, or what I would have to go through to stay clean.

I do know when I promised to never touch a drink or drug, I meant it from the purest place in my heart.

I am forever grateful to the counselors who worked with me to stay sober and gave me the tools I needed to make it out of there with confidence. The two men and an amazing woman who spent their time with me changed my life forever. It was no accident I ended up on their doorstep, lost and looking for direction. What I then thought was the most humiliating and worst day of my life was the start of an entirely new life I could not even fathom.

What I had to cope with in my first year of sobriety was an emotional odyssey, textured with a flood of diverse feelings unknown to me in years. It was a nightmare I had to live out without substances to hide behind. This time, I would be entirely present to witness and feel the ramifications of the many hurtful decisions I had made.

Couldn't Stay Clean

Shortly after I completed rehab, I was advised that living with my landlord was no longer safe if I wanted to stay sober. She was still using, and Jack and I both were doing our best to stay substance-free. We started looking for a new place but the right rental eluded us. Jack tried to complete the same outpatient program I had, but his poor attitude and ego held him back. He remained sober but refused to go to meetings or work with a sponsor. He tried to find a job, but it never lasted more than a few weeks.

I stayed as close as possible to my sponsor, counselor and the meetings. I was not exactly sure what I was doing, but I knew the people who had been sober for some time had a positive influence on my life, and I wanted what they had. I wanted to be a better person in my pursuit of happiness.

In my fourth month of sobriety, I got a call at work from my landlord. She said there was a problem, and she needed to talk with me when I got home. It turned out Jack had stolen some things from her, and she found them in our room. Also, he had been drinking all day and fell down the stairs. I was shaking, so angry and disappointed. He was the person who introduced me to the idea of getting clean, and now he had jumped ship. We were supposed to stay sober and have a sensible life together; it would not work if only one of us stayed clean. I found Jack outside, smoking a cigarette and stumbling around. He smelled like whiskey and dirt. He said I looked mad. I made a huge, angry scene, crying and yelling. What he had done was unacceptable, and I was unwilling to have anything to do with this behavior. Then I saw it. Hazed look. Pupils small as pinheads. Eyes disconnected and vacant. Under the influence and absent from reality. I knew what he was feeling all too well, but now it was different. I was able to envision what I had been like under the influence. Talking to him was useless because, even if he could hear me talking, his mind was shut off. All he cared about was getting fucked up, and nothing I could do or say would change his mind. All I could hope for was to try and talk to him when he started sobering up.

Within a couple of weeks, he was back to doing heroin all day and stealing from me. I tried to keep it a secret, fearful of what my sponsor would say. As this went on for a few months, one of my friends from rehab advised me to tell my sponsor because the situation could be dangerous to my recovery. I agreed and clued my sponsor in. She told me I needed to be strong and set a solid boundary if I wanted this relationship to work. I truly did, and I loved Jack very much. She advised he needed to succeed in a sober-living home for six months, and if he completed the six months, we would go from there.

Jack was irked at first and did not want to go to the sober-living facility. After a few days, he agreed, and I helped him move into the sober house. I thought it best that I take the opportunity to relocate as well. I asked if I could move home temporarily. My parents agreed. They said I could stay in my brother's room since he was stationed in Italy with the Navy. I could bring only what I needed; the rest would go to storage. So I packed up my stuff. Friends helped me move, and I was gone.

Time passed, and Jack made it to five months in the sober-living home. I was hopeful, looking for apartments we could call home. My sponsor told me there was one more part of this boundary: Jack had to show me he was dedicated to this relationship. I was heartbroken and disappointed, but I had to trust her opinion. I let him know, and surprisingly, he took it well.

A week later, he told me he wanted to show me something. He drove me out near the beach to one of the homes his parents owned. The house had a musky scent and too many cats. We took a tour. He had been working on fixing some things around the house, which would be vacated as soon as the current tenants left. As we looked around the backyard, he asked what I thought. I said it was a nice house. He asked if I wanted to move into the house with him, and I was stunned. This was his way of showing commitment. I was beyond excited. When I told my parents, they were leery of the idea. My mom was always hesitant about Jack. She did not think he was a good match for me.

Part of the agreement was that we help renovate the home. We sanded all the floors and painted every room. It took us a month or so. We put in a lot of hard work; and when it was finished, the house was perfect. His parents wanted us to rent out the spare rooms to other sober tenants. It was a four-bedroom house. We had a larger room and two smaller rooms for rent. The larger room went to an odd couple: a 42-year-old woman and her 22-year-old boyfriend. We tried not to judge, but this was not your traditional boyfriend and girlfriend. Then, there was a kind, elderly Hispanic woman who had a couple of screws loose. The last room went to another elder gentleman who played music and had been sober a very long time. He was the peacekeeper in the house.

Shortly after moving in, we got a golden retriever named Doc. He was my baby, and I loved him with all of my heart. I got a job nearby at a barbershop specializing in quick, men's haircuts. The theme was pretty girls in sporty outfits. It was not where I wanted to be, but one of my past employers had opened up another store and gave me a second chance because of my sobriety. When I worked for her before, I was a mess. I came to work with physical evidence of an abusive relationship, not to mention I was as high as a kite; so it was with optimism which I greeted this new opportunity. But the optimism did not last.

Jack had gotten a construction job nearby and seemed to be doing well. Once we had been in the house for a few months, though, he relapsed again. I tried attending the meetings near our house, but I just did not fit in. With Jack using, I would need to stay close to my usual support group, which meant driving more than an hour each night to attend meetings in the town where I began my recovery.

One of the nights I got home, Doc seemed distraught. I found Jack in our master bathroom. Blood covered Jack and the bathroom fixtures. He was so high, barely alert, and he was muttering something amid the chaos. I dragged him to the bed and laid him down. His wrist had a deep cut, at least a half-inch deep and three-inches wide. It appeared as though it had stopped bleeding, and Jack was probably all right other than the amount of blood loss. I returned to the bathroom, pondering what I would do next.

I stared at the bathroom for a long time. I was paralyzed. What was I going to do? Should I call the police, or his parents? Should I tell the roommates? This exact moment in my life was what my counselor called a behavioral relapse. In fear, I did what I did best. I hid. I pretended the whole thing never happened. His relapse, the suicide attempt. I stayed up all night, cleaning the blood from the bathroom. Afterward, I sat in the shower and broke down while Jack was passed out in the bed. Then, I got up the next morning and went to work. I did not say anything to him about the relapse or our bloody secret. I did the same thing I had done when I was raped. I did my best to ignore it and pretend it never happened.

I wish I would have known then what I know now. You cannot hide your demons because eventually they will destroy you, especially when you are sober. I stayed substance-free, but I awoke every day hating myself and my life just as I did while using. Jack had become my new drug. I was addicted to our relationship in an unhealthy way. I wanted us to end up happily ever after, despite his inability to stay sober and his lack of consideration for my well-being. It was possibly the most toxic situation I have ever been in. I was focused on the ring on my finger, our house and our dog. From the outside, it looked perfect; and somewhere in my mind, I was convinced it would all work out. Since I was little, I held onto the "white picket fence" idea. I wanted to get married and have a house and family. After the death of my baby, all I wanted was a second chance at being a mother. If I wanted to have that opportunity, I would need someone to fill the father role. With Jack, it would be like sticking a square peg in a round hole. Jack would never fit the role of being a husband and father. But I was desperate to make my dream come true. Even in sobriety, I clung to denial. Whether Jack was right for me or not was not my concern. I thought somehow he would end up being right, fitting into my poorly thought-out plan of building a family of my own.

But everything started to fall apart. The bizarre relationship of the older woman and the young boyfriend began unraveling when she relapsed and started drinking again. The eviction notice I served them triggered a sequence that is among the most stressful 30 days of my life. The boyfriend moved out before she did. She started fistfights with me, yelled at me in her drunken rages, drove drunk and began smoking cigarettes in the house.

I started losing my composure at work from the stress at home. In my sobriety, I noticed the owner of the shop where I worked was not at all who I thought she was. Much worse, she held fast to a resentment from my previous employment with her. She hated me. I hated going to work, and I hated coming home.

Jack started pawning our belongings: laptops, flat screens, even car parts. Nothing in our home was off-limits. He started disappearing for a day or two at first, then weeks. He went on drug binges, then came home and started crazy fights. He took the tenants' rent checks and cashed them, so the mortgage was unpaid. He tried to kill himself every so often, whether it was an overdose, or cutting himself open.

The only thing that stayed consistent was my sobriety. I went to a meeting five days a week and called my sponsor every day. I told her a lot of the truth of what was going on. But not the whole truth.

Eventually my boss tried to demote me. I was lost and felt like I had nothing left, much like the day I decided to get sober. I played with the thought of relapsing because I felt sorry for myself, but instead, I called my sponsor. She said to take the next step. I went online and started applying for jobs. The very next day, I went to an interview at a salon with better pay and a better environment. I was hired on the spot, but the salon was far from my house. Conveniently, it was only 10 minutes from my parents' house. This seemed to be a sign.

A week later, I sat in the driveway, as I had every night for months, frightened to go inside and see what setbacks awaited me. I called my sponsor and said, "I don't know what I'm doing." I went on about how much I hated Jack for all of the things he had done.

That I hated my home because it had become such a scary place in my world. Ultimately, I was extremely unhappy. I was sobbing and shaking. Then she asked, "What do you think God is telling you to do?" I did not think. I just blurted out, "Leave."

So that is what I did; I went inside. The house was quiet. Jack was not there, and whatever roommates remained were locked away in their rooms. I felt weak, like maybe I should just sleep on it. Maybe in time things would work out. Then I got a text message from my mom: "We're worried about you, maybe you should come home." I was being told what to do by God or the universe, or something much bigger than me, so I packed what I could; and I left.

Again, I rented a storage unit and moved back into my brother's room. Jack's mom kept Doc the wonder dog. I was so sad that it had to be that way, but I was not sure where I would end up; and she had the means of giving him a good life and home. I will never be able to thank Jack's parents enough for all they did for us while we were together. Without his mom, I would have been too afraid to walk into my first meeting. She helped me more in my first year's sobriety than anyone. She was a vital part of the team of people who kept me clean.

Jack and I do not speak anymore. I think we both knew we could not be in each other's lives. I did not say goodbye or clarify that our relationship was over. I took off my ring and covered a tattoo of our anniversary date. I felt he should already know why I was leaving. After all I had swallowed, there was nothing more I could say. However, I am grateful he showed me how strong I can be, and why I do not use drugs anymore. One would think I learned my lessons not to date guys who clearly needed fixing. Unfortunately, that was not the case. Jack was just the beginning of my new addiction to men who needed help. I believe addiction and low self-esteem go hand-in-hand. While my mind and body were free of substances, my heart was fearful of being alone. Guys who had problems needed someone who was stable like me. I needed them to avoid loneliness. In focusing on others, I was able to avoid focusing on what still needed to be changed within me.

Falling For A Monster

After I broke it off with Jack, I attended more meetings than ever. They were a safe place to gather my thoughts, and I always heard something useful or motivational. My mentality at the time was that I should date someone who was also in recovery. I worried that if I dated someone who was not, they would not understand my sobriety, or perhaps, they would push me to drink or use drugs.

I stayed close with Clair and her boyfriend. Clair had a solid relationship and a new outlook on life. Two girls who once did drugs together were now sober friends, who could depend on each other for support. Her boyfriend lived in a sober-living house with a guy named Ted. Ted was tall, handsome, smart, motivated and only sober a short time.

Ted and I started dating and spent a lot of time with Clair and her boyfriend. No one knew Ted very well because he recently moved from a different town. Early in our relationship, Clair joked that he could be a killer or criminal, and no one would ever know since we knew so little about him. Her statement was funny at the time but turned out to be less funny than anyone could have imagined.

After only four months of dating, Ted wanted us to get an apartment. My better judgment declared it an awful idea, but he was manipulative. He convinced me we would get married and would be together forever. In our early days, he was kind and gentle. He called often and made me believe he genuinely cared about me. He was a master at acting and making himself seem to be something he was not.

Danny was my tattoo artist and "big brother." Although he was not biologically related to me, he had been in my life since I was 16. When I was using, he made sure I was cared for and had a place to eat and sleep. When I got clean, he told me he also was sober. He had been for 10 years. He never pushed me into sobriety or mentioned his own battles because he knew I needed my own journey and time to learn what addiction had to teach me. When I got clean, he was ecstatic! He celebrated my milestones and made sure I always knew he was proud of me.

I had never taken anyone I was dating to meet my big brother before. But, blinded by infatuation, I decided to take Ted to meet Danny. I brought Ted to get tattooed, but Danny did not like Ted at all. He said that Ted seemed arrogant and manipulative. This made me leery because I trusted Danny's judgment. But my fascination for Ted was genuine, and I made the decision to move in with him, despite the premonitions that this would be a doomed relationship.

A month later, Danny was shot and killed by police. While it remains unclear why they needed to kill him, they did. The police report stated that police had stopped his truck and attempted to ask what he was doing driving up into the mountains. They reported that Danny seemed distressed and took off. They chased him to a dead end where he then exited the vehicle and pulled a gun on the officers. They shot him and killed him. Amphetamines reportedly were present in his toxicology tests.

When I got sober, I mentally prepared myself for anything I thought might happen. Maybe a friend overdosing or someone I loved dying in a car crash. But not this. The severity and intensity of Danny's death broke my heart. I felt so vulnerable. My big brother was always a phone call away. His tattoo shop was my sanctuary, a place I could always go to find peace and wisdom. A place where I was safe. Now I felt alone. I was broken up for months. I hardly spoke to anyone. When Danny died, light was shed on his overlapping relationships with two women and the children he fathered with them. I knew both women and their beautiful babies—one girl and one boy. I was unaware that Danny had been seeing both of them and was living a double life. But I am fortunate to have relationships with both women and their children.

While struggling with Danny's death, Ted displayed one of the first warning signs of his selfishness. He would not go to the funeral, and he was put off by my grieving. I thought maybe it was just his way of dealing with death. Some people do not deal with it as well as others, and maybe the severity of the situation left him feeling uncomfortable. In reality, there was nothing Ted could do or say to make me feel better about losing Danny.

Ted had a brother who also was battling addiction and doing his best to remain sober. Ted wanted to help his brother and asked that he move in with us, and I agreed. His brother's name was Dean, and I loved having him with us. Dean was like a little brother to me, and I valued our relationship. He was wise, spiritual and humble, much different from Ted. He was, by far, one of the most positive people I have ever known. Always smiling, and making the most out of life.

Over time, Ted and I started fighting a lot. Mostly about money. He made a lot more than I did but did not contribute to any of the bills. We split the rent, and that was it. If ever I asked him for help, he would ask why I had not paid it already. The bills were my responsibility and not his.

Ted was nothing short of a monster. He was mean, controlling and hateful. Once he became comfortable, he dropped the act of being kind and considerate. He became unbearably demanding. He expected lunch and dinner to be ready for him on weekdays; breakfast on the weekends. I was expected to clean and do the laundry every week. All toiletries and groceries were to be stocked at all times, or he would reprimand me. Something was severely wrong with him. He mocked me every day and made me feel bad about myself. He questioned my clothes, hair color and makeup choices, stating I was making myself look sleazy. He had serious control and self-esteem issues. I began feeling worse than I did while living with Jack.

My family hated him, and he was not allowed at my parents' house at all. Any time I saw my mother, she begged me to break up with him, echoing the exact thing Danny warned me about—his manipulation. I helped Ted build his life, buy a car and bolster his credit with his part of the apartment rent. By this time,

Ted owed me a substantial amount of money. I had supplied the down-payment on his car, helped pay his phone bill and other expenses.

Ted's anger was extreme. One night he made me cry, and he got angry when I did not quiet down quickly enough. He jumped out of bed, ripped the lamp out of the wall and threw it at my face. He missed by an inch. From there, he yelled at me—so close our noses almost touched—and dared me to make one more sound, or "I'll throw you through the wall." I stopped eating and sleeping after that night. I was afraid to leave, and afraid to stay.

I had to leave one time when I was asked to be the main speaker at the local meeting hall. I was nervous because I had never spoken for 45 minutes. Ted was out somewhere, which was good for me. I never asked him where he was or for any details because I was afraid he would belittle me. When I got to the meeting, many seemed out of sorts. They were uneasily giving me weird looks or avoiding me. I finally asked one of my friends about the odd behavior. He told me Ted was seen across the way at a bar, and he was with one of the girls known for her slutty reputation. I could hardly breathe. Now, he added cheating to our troubled relationship.

I kept my poise and spoke well despite my broken heart and scattered mind. A group of friends came home to make sure I was all right. The friends I made in sobriety were the most genuine and kind people I know. They stocked the apartment with root beer, ice cream and licorice. One of the girls even bought flowers, doing her best to help me feel better. We watched a movie before they left. I waited for the confrontation when Ted got home. When Ted showed up, he was infuriated. He denied the infidelity and began breaking things. I knew as I sat there this relationship had been over for a long time. Ted had no feelings for me. He only wanted to exploit my financial stability and to sponge an independent life off me. I was nothing but a paycheck and housekeeper.

Later in the night, Ted tried to apologize, suggested we start over and make it work. Dean loved his brother, but Ted treated him as poorly as he did me. Dean privately told me this relationship would never improve, that Ted would never see himself as the monster he was. Nothing good would ever come of this relationship, and I was a better person than Ted. Dean said I deserved more, that I should leave and never look back. Dean was honest. He did not want to hurt Ted, but he wanted to stop both of us from continuing this abusive cycle. Dean left first. He went to a sober-living house where he did not have to hear constant arguing and crying.

A week later, I sat in the very place Ted and I often went to be alone before we had the apartment. It was a small parking lot that was always empty. We often went there and talked for hours enjoying each other's company. In the silence of the night, I realized our relationship was strikingly similar to that of the parking lot: Empty. He was a money-hungry cheater who wanted to suck me dry of everything I had. He was already in debt to me for thousands of dollars. I needed to get out.

The next morning I waited as he got ready for work. I had been sleeping on the couch regularly for some time. When he came out of the room to leave, I told him I was leaving him. He had no emotion and just nodded in agreement.

I packed what I could into my small car. As I went back inside, I realized all of these "things" were meaningless. Except for my clothes, a few family heirlooms and some knickknacks, all of these possessions were just memories of bad men. Jack and Ted were part of all of them, so I left them all there. I moved home. This time I got my own room. It had an office and a lot of space. I asked to stay until I published my first book. My parents were happy to have me home safely and assured me I could stay as long as I needed.

Ted became lonely and wanted to get back together, but I had more ambition for my life than supporting a six-foot, two-inch baby. His ambition of having that wedding came to fruition as he quickly found a girlfriend, moved her in and married her within 90 days. I think he was happy, and maybe that was what mattered. Ted and his new wife used my debit card information to open online accounts within a few months of their marriage. I pressed charges and have been working with a detective to make sure they are brought to justice.

My most important lesson in these two relationships was accountability. I got exactly what I signed up for. I found scumbags, and I paid for it. A good friend called it "putting lipstick on a pig." The beauty was superficial and almost comical. No matter what I tried to do to make these guys better, it was not up to me. Ted would never be anything short of a controlling, narcissistic, violent monster. With his collection of crimes, I can only hope his freedom is short-lived, as society would be better off without him. Jack and Ted were the perfect examples of what happens when you substitute one addiction for another.

My first book was about dating, not on how much I claim to know, but many of the things I have done wrong and failed to notice like dangerous characteristics in a mate and what is unhealthy in a relationship. I think dating and addiction have an effect on one another. Poor self-esteem and heartbreak left people looking for an outlet to banish pain. My goal was to prevent that from happening. My motivation? Perhaps if younger girls new to dating were more aware of what was out there and what an unhealthy relationship looked like, they would mow over the assholes and find a decent guy. I put my experience openly into the world so maybe it will act as a preventative. I think it is also important for people to have something they can relate to. Having an unsuccessful relationship is embarrassing. Perhaps reading about someone who has experienced the same, and come out stronger, will motivate others not to be so hard on themselves. Having someone who they can relate to is productive in making people discover their worth.

Ted and Jack seemed like a toxic disease I would have to suffer until the end of time. Today I know they were nothing short of steppingstones. I can only hope that sharing what has helped me will help others eliminate the chances of someone, such as Ted, taking advantage of other innocent people. Exposing these situations helps to ensure that being treated this way is unacceptable.

Why Did I Do it?

This is the question everyone is dying to have me answer. Why did I choose to use drugs? It is simple: I was a selfish coward, and I enjoyed the effects produced by drugs and alcohol. I blamed the world for every horrible thing that happened. From getting raped three times to the death of my unborn child. I was so disgustingly selfish that I honestly felt these things were being done to me, and I had no part in it.

I guess my first mistake was hiding the first rape at age 12. A trauma like that was too harrowing for a preteenager to deal with alone. I should have told my parents the truth and sought counseling. Looking back at my life and examining my actions, I can conclude soberly that the thoughts I chose to clutter my mind with were so toxic and untrue that I lost my grasp of reality. In being raped, I felt alone, when really that is what I chose to be. I was afraid that when someone found out what had happened to me, I would have to sit in a courtroom in front of strangers and explain how my virginity was beaten and robbed from me in a tent somewhere in Utah. I believed my parents would be disappointed, and I valued their opinion.

It was the power of corrupt thinking. The girl in camp who offered the crazy advice that rape was normal invited my innocent mind to think that being taken advantage of was acceptable. In no way am I saying this is an excuse for being a junkie. I can only assume that this is when my obscured thinking began.

Why do people do drugs? Because we are drama queens who like attention, especially that of a negative nature. It is a giant show, and we are cast in the leading roles. We are infamous for being lost on a path of destruction. I do not believe addiction is a disease. I do think that environment can lead to risky behavior. For example, if parents are practicing addicts, that environment could lead children to follow in their footsteps. I do not feel there was anything genetically programmed in my brain that made drugs or alcohol irresistible. If anything, my parents taught me the exact opposite. I was a rebel and challenged everything they said. My addiction simply came from being a free thinker. I am a visual, curious person. I wanted to know why something was "bad." So much so, that even when warned of the danger, I would do it anyway. I wanted to find out myself. I lacked trust in the opinions and judgment of others, especially authority figures. *I was selfish and self-centered to the fullest extent.* That is why I became an alcohol-infused heroin junkie.

There is no good reason why I did these things. I felt sorry for myself. When Berta left, I felt sorry for myself. When I was raped, I felt sorry for myself. And so on, and so forth with every "tragedy" I withstood. I built up this resentment at the world for things from which I ultimately could have coped and moved on. Instead, I chose to hold fast to grudges and sorrow.

Everyone in the world has tragedy. Everyone weathers things that are unfair. It is how we choose to deal with it that holds power over our lives. I played a huge part in everything that happened to me. In fact, I put myself in those situations willingly. That is why I find it comical when people demand sympathy or claim their lives are "unfair." It is their perception that causes them to believe that. I went into that tent *knowing* it was an unwise idea. I continued a relationship, physically and emotionally, with Stan *knowing* he was selfish. I went to parties with lowlife criminals capable of rape *knowing* I was in danger. I had sex with Zeek, time after time, *knowing* I was not on birth control and, even if the possibility was low, I could get pregnant. I overdosed in the bathroom *knowing* I probably would not die, but my baby surely would. I willingly drank and used drugs *knowing* it was the road to perdition, the last stop for a pathetic junkie.

My No. 1 problem was me. I chose to hide behind drugs and alcohol instead of pulling my head out of my ass and doing something with my life. By chance, I found sobriety and a sponsor who was as tough as nails. She told me to knock the pout off my face and stop feeling sorry for myself. That my bad attitude and lifelong tragedy was of my own creation. I decided to take her advice and make something of myself. Luckily for me, not one person in Alcoholics Anonymous or my rehab felt sorry for me. Every one of them called me on my bullshit. I was humiliated and embarrassed, but it was OK. Feeling that way was part of the process.

There are no words to describe how I feel reading this book knowing I chose to do all of these things to myself and the people I loved. From the first cigarette, to the first drink, the first drug, it was *all* a choice. One bad choice after another led me to a life no one would ever want to live. I am thankful to everyone who broke me down and exposed me for the deplorable wretch I was. I am not the one who suffered most from being a junkie. My family was emotionally spent, exiled to a place to which they had to disown me. And I thank them from the bottom of my heart for kicking me out of my house. My behavior could have influenced my siblings, and my parents did the right thing by forcing me out.

Today I have rebuilt the life I destroyed. I have my family back. I help other rape victims and encourage them to be strong. I work with addicts and their families, promising that a better, sober life is possible. For the most part, I have cleaned up the mess I made. With that said, I do suffer things from which I will never recover.

I am pained every day when I think about my baby. I miss it terribly, and I am disgusted with myself in knowing I sacrificed my child for drug addiction. I work as hard as possible to build a solid foundation with the hopes that one day I will be granted a second chance at being a mother, a chance I am fully aware I do not deserve. I can thank addiction for a debilitating, embarrassing opiate-induced brain disorder. In a moment, I can lose all the daily functions I took for granted. Such as my speech and movement of my limbs. Accompanied by the excruciating physical pain I hid from for five years. This is an actual disease, but it stemmed from a choice to use opiates as recreational drugs.

Finally, the nightmares. I do not sleep often. Most nights I sleep an average of two to four hours. When I am awake, I am in control of my thoughts. I am of sound mind, and I have come a long way. However, the terrible things I have done and the places I have been are as alive in my dreams as they were at the times they happened. I have physically beaten boyfriends in my sleep when reliving one of the three rapes in a nightmare. Sometimes I dream about the decaying living room full of bodies, some dead, where I willingly sat and used heroin. The life I chose to live is absolutely horrible and morally reprehensible. But that is the point; it was *my choice*. Despite the burdens I live with from my experience as a junkie, I choose today to use my knowledge to help others from going down the same path. I fear the nighttime, knowing what flashbacks may come. But I am grateful to be alive, and I am fully aware that I am responsible for what has happened. I learned the hard way that feeling sorry for myself is fruitless. So, no matter what, I *refuse* to get lost in self-pity.

My Second Chance

I learned much throughout my addiction. Maybe I even learned most of it in sobriety. I think I played the victim as an excuse to prolong my drug use. Perhaps to make people feel sorry for me, and hang around people who were just as sick as I was. I convinced myself I did not deserve better. That doing drugs and slowly killing myself was the existence meant for me.

When I had about six months' sobriety, I began to respect myself. I discovered I can have anything I want. As long as I am sober, there is no dream beyond my grasp. In working with my sponsor, I was accountable for my actions, the choices I made were my own; and I could hold no one else responsible for anything.

After I dumped Ted and moved home, I ran into an old friend from high school. He had done pretty well for himself, and we dated about a month. I learned a lot from him. Although it did not work out, he taught me what it was like to be treated well. He was kind and giving, and I was entirely happy. He complemented my life. There were no problems, expectations or stress; he did not seek anything except my company. In dating this man, I learned I had been settling for boys in my previous relationships.

I recently had a boyfriend for a couple of months and cut it off because he had no ambitions. I found it is not superficial to have standards. I like being treated nicely while dating someone with ambitions and goals. For the time being, I have chosen to remain single.

That is probably the most responsible decision for now.

When I got sober, I attended meetings regularly. I was one of the faces people counted on to be there. When I had nine months, my counselor invited me to an event that a local nonprofit was holding to raise awareness of heroin addiction. There was a panel, all about my age, but they had been sober much longer. Five minutes before it started, my counselor told me to sit with the panel. He wanted me to tell my story to a roomful of strangers. I pleaded I could not, and he reassured me that I could.

I dislike public speaking, but I did what he asked. Ever since that night, I was asked to speak many times. First, it was at rehabs, then high schools; now it is town hall meetings with the mayor and police chief. I lead other speakers at the schools, and I have surprised myself by being the featured speaker at various conventions.

I never thought I would do this, and I still do not enjoy it; but I know spreading the message is more important than my fear of speaking. No matter how nervous, I always attend if asked; and I tell the story you have read in this memoir. I hope it will prevent people from using drugs. I want to shed light on the truth of addiction: That it is a frightening choice and a doomed fate. I also find it important for people to know if they go down the wrong path and want to turn their lives around, there are people who can help. No matter what it is, it is never too late to get clean and change your life. I am not sure how long speaking will be a career option, but for the time being, I will do my best to enjoy it. I think it is a privilege to have an opportunity to make a difference.

The most relevant aspect of speaking is what happens behind the scenes. When I go to high schools, the kids could care less that I am there. They think sobriety is silly. They think I do not know anything. Before leaving, I always end with the same warning: "I hope *never* to see you in a rehab or a meeting, because if I do, then my message wasn't delivered."

Over the time I have spoken at many schools, I have seen some of these same kids under different circumstances. When I get to see them a second time, they are hardly the kid I saw sitting behind a desk. By now, they are broken and filled with drugs, anxiety and fear. When they recognize me, the first thing they say is, "You were right." It breaks my heart to hear this. I sometimes get down on myself. I speculate on what other words I could have said to stop them from putting a needle in their arm. But we are all entitled to our own journey, our own dignity to fail. These kids have to learn the hard way, and the harsh truth is that some of them are going to die. Some of them will ultimately be a statistic, an example that drugs are a quick killer, and no one is guaranteed to survive.

My life today is better than anything I would have pictured. I never would have thought that at three years' sober, I would be a public speaker, published author and a successful hair stylist. I enjoy this time in my life and have the things I have always dreamed of having.

At 19, I started writing *The Game: Wholehearted*. Six years later, I self-published it in hopes of finding a mainstream publisher for this book. Within two months of printing *The Game*, Rachel Zarrella from Immortal Publishing contacted me and wanted to produce *Junkie*, although it was then in its infancy.

I have a full-time editor who is extremely generous. I have searched through a great number of editors, only to see them destroy my work and put me down. I edited my first book on my own because I had given up hope. Then I met my editor, Larry Jones. He speaks my language and enjoys my writing. I can send him anything, and it is as if we have the same set of eyes, except his are better with spelling and grammar. More than my editor, he is my friend. He is also sober and shares bits of his recovery with me. Larry is my gift from God, nothing short of my very own angel. Without him, none of this would be possible. I am grateful for him each day, and if I can help it, *no one* else will ever edit my work.

My family had to do what was best for them and was justified to cut me off. While I was using, I wrote my mother some cruel emails: ugly things about her and my entire family. While I was not of sane mind, I regret this so much. Those words still hurt my mother today. She is thrilled about how far I have come; however, I cannot erase the memories of who I was. Part of being clean is living to show my family I love them, while treating them as they deserve to be treated. I have worked extremely hard at developing a relationship with each of my family members, and I do whatever I can to keep those relationships growing. I am extremely grateful for my siblings and parents.

My twin sister, afraid to take my calls for five years, asked me to stand by her side at her wedding as the maid of honor. Even now, I am in tears, awed at the power of her request.

Today I know how much my family loves me. When I do not come home at night, they do not worry. They hope maybe I found a decent man to date, but they are not afraid I might have nodded off in a car, overdosing somewhere. And that is just remarkable.

I have not shared these facts of my life with any family members, and they will only learn of them if they read this book. I hope they, and other readers, can understand these words were written to promote awareness. Today I am not those things I have done, those people I have hurt or those lies I have told. These things do not make me tough or intimidating. They hold no power. What I did before I was sober are the actions of a coward. A scared, little girl who wanted to be right and threw away five years of her life to heroin and alcohol. I thought drugs were cool once. I thought the lifestyle was rebellious and interesting. I was wrong. Nothing, not one thing I did when I was high, was ever cool. Everything I did affected someone in a negative way, but mostly I harmed myself. Drugs showed me how quickly you can change when brain functions compete with opiates.

I have yet to meet anyone who is a successful junkie. Nothing about addiction is fun. No addict I know has a life worth living. My second chance is something I treasure and will protect at all costs. Without my sobriety, I have nothing. If I choose to go back to drugs and alcohol, all of the things I have will vanish. I will destroy the life I love, the life I worked so hard to build. I did not create this empire, full of my hopes and dreams, only to tear it down.

Recovery

When I first got clean, I strongly relied on the Alcoholics Anonymous and Narcotics Anonymous programs. As their names implied, members were anonymous, but there was a gray area of what was, and was not, allowed to be shared outside meetings. With that said, I do not agree with it. I respect the programs and what they teach. Without them, I would not be where I am now. The 12 steps and work with my sponsor have been the most productive things in my growth. The 12 steps are like the 10 commandments in helping you evolve into a decent human being. People in the rooms, or my "fellows" in recovery, have helped me and still do.

When I first got sober, which I have talked about throughout this book, I went to many meetings and activities based on sobriety or recovery. Three years later, I have likes and dislikes about the one-day-at-a-time programs. Like anonymity. I think it is ridiculous to hide from society, or not promote, something as valuable as AA and NA fellowship. But most meetings are readily available if you look them up online or by phone. Depending on where you go and the people there, the atmosphere of each meeting will vary. That is part of why I no longer attend meetings.

What used to be productive and inspirational has turned into a pity party. I think it is great that younger people are finding out about recovery and attending meetings, but some are forced to be there. Instead of learning from people who have been sober a long time, there is a chorus of whining about how hard life is. Then they deny accountability, claiming to suffer from the "disease" of addiction. Which you know I disagree with entirely. As I have written repetitively, drug and alcohol use is a choice. The one thing a using junkie, or counterproductive sober addict relishes the most is an excuse. Saying that addiction is a disease is the very excuse that gets them off the hook. It fulfills their need to take the focus off them. The meetings will always be there, and I still go to take cakes marking my annual sobriety anniversaries. I also go to support others, and to show people just starting out that it is possible to stay clean. For a lot of people who go to meetings, sometimes they take a break for a while. Maybe that is what I am doing.

More than being sober, I took a commitment much bigger than meetings. My best friend in the world has chosen to be Straight Edge for the rest of life. When I got clean, I saw people come in and out of the rooms. Relapsing over and over. I felt like, although AA and NA do their best to prevent it, it is tolerated there. So I did more research on seriously committing to becoming Edge and being a part of that community. I took my commitment to Edge with honor and respect. Edge is for life. I have pledged to stay pure until death. I wear this title with the utmost pride, and that is what works for me.

I also know people who have found sanctuary in church or religion. All I have come to know is that in getting clean, rehab and meetings will save your life. They are the tools you need to build a foundation for a life worth living. If you can go into the process willingly, you will find a better way of life. After you have some sobriety time, you will find that different methods work for different people. If you want to maintain your sobriety, you have to find the right one for you. I know of people who have gone to numerous meetings a week for more than 50 years, and that is what it takes for them. In no way, shape or form am I trying to endorse one way over another. I am simply saying what has worked for me. I love the meetings and all of the people I have come to know. But, for now, sitting in the midst of negative newcomers is counterproductive. That, and I simply lack enough patience to be part of it. If and when I do go to a meeting, I will choose one with regulars who own solid recovery, people who have been sober for a very long time and use the time in a meeting room to discuss solutions, not self-pity. Newcomers are, by far, the most important people in the rooms because they literally are attempting to save their own lives.

There are heroes in AA and NA who are capable of guiding them. I am of a different nature. I do not find shame in admitting my addiction. I think the whole world should accept its mistakes and calmly own up to them. I speak at schools about choices and addiction. Not recovery. My voice is about prevention and education. The teachers tell me they appreciate my honesty. Also, there is no question a student can ask that I will not answer. I respond with truth in its rawest, grittiest form.

Recovery is important, for we can all learn from it. There are different things that help junkies find new lives. AA and NA open the doors to find out what works best for each person. Find people who live a life you want to live and learn from them. Beyond anything else, commit to being clean and sober. Whatever the cost, continue to live your life this way. *No matter what!*

To The Addict

Addiction is the only dependency that convinces you that you are not dependent.

The entire time I was using, I was truly convinced I did not have a problem. I just thought I knew how to party harder than everyone else. There is nothing about the word "heroin" that is not serious. Heroin is by far the worst drug in existence.

It is important for me to make clear that I started with marijuana and alcohol. Being slightly older, I have grasped that an adolescent who drinks or uses drugs on an everyday basis is far from normal. In some way, we all want to be accepted, to fit in. We grow up with this idea that we need to stand out among our peers. However, we may go about it the wrong way. There is something in all of us that is unique, some quality at which we naturally excel. Instead of focusing on that special trait, we can get stuck in what the media portray as cool or romantic, usually suggesting the party scene is the place to be.

I know for me, I thought being tough was cool. I enjoyed that people were intimidated by me. That they feared saying the wrong thing, or I might act out violently. It was a sick sense of control I was after, not understanding it was a warped perception that had control of me. Being tough or feared is not cool; it is a form of isolation.

There once was a time when drug use was unacceptable. The kids who abused them were considered lost. Kids respected their parents enough to trust their judgment. It seems as if the main goal for this generation is for the child to control the parent. To challenge every rule, every piece of advice. Our parents are so valuable to us; they have much more experience at life. They know why being a certain way or doing destructive things will hurt our potential.

When I go to high schools or events to speak, there is always a group of kids with intimidating stares, burning eyes glaring, ready to challenge everything I know. Their eyes tell me they are going to do whatever the fuck they want. I was that arrogant once, and look where it got me. Of all the things I could change, I wish I would have listened more. I did not have to make careless decisions that led to addiction. But I thought I knew better.

Whether you have already been in treatment or not, the one thing every addict needs to know is that it *is* a choice. While many say it is a disease, I know better and dispute that argument. As someone who has medical conditions, I can assure you I did not go to a dealer and ask for cancer. Nor did I ask the doctor to write me a prescription for a brain disorder. If we get stuck in substances, we are paralyzed in a self-loathing process. We blame everything and everyone but ourselves for our predicament. You are the one slamming the needle into your vein, the bottle in your mouth, or the pills between your teeth. A very important thing I gleaned in recovery is I am the only one who can be held responsible for my actions. I create thoughts that become actions. Once I act out, I cannot take it back. While what you have done cannot be erased, how you act in the future can be adjusted. My attitude, ego and low self-esteem contributed to me becoming a junkie. I did not give myself a chance. Instead of trying to work on the parts of me I did not like, I hid behind a piece of foil.

You can change. While substances are a hard thing to do away with, *you* are the only one who can change your life. If you decide to spend the night disposing of your stash and paraphernalia, while committing to waking up tomorrow ready for detox; then that is what will happen. You are stronger than you know.

In my first year of sobriety, I impressed myself. I was able to admit I knew nothing of how to be a decent human being. How I was choosing to live was not working. So I became observant. I was drawn to people who lived lives I admired. I became brave enough to ask them for advice. The angry, little junkie became an empty slate, and I had an opportunity to reinvent myself. For the first time in my life, I understood I could be anything I wanted to be. I took note of the qualities I valued in others and did my best to be a good combination of them all.

It was my new project. When I was using, every day was a project. Arranging money, picking up drugs, stealing, using in secrecy, lying and hurting people. So I chose to change it. I cannot stand people who play the victim. Why not be an example of strength instead of an overplayed sob story? It seems the one thing most people lack is ambition. There is no limit to what we are able to become. Let go of your excuses and eliminate the ball and chain holding you down.

I invite you to give yourself a chance to be the person you have always dreamed of being. Surrender and ask the sky to guide you onto a path that will take you where you want to go. Offer yourself to the world as an unfilled vessel. You can add and subtract whatever traits you wish. Remember, you are in control. No one can stop you. All you have to do is keep moving forward.

I can assure you within my early sobriety, I never imagined I would be three years' sober with three careers which are advancing every minute. When I was a kid, I used to love library day. I once looked at all the books and authors' names and dreamed one day I would grow up to be an author, and my name would be on the book that some little girl excitedly borrowed from the very same library.

Maybe I had to become a monster fueled by substances to comprehend that my dreams did not have to be just dreams. That by breaking the cycle, dreams could become goals. That with a clear mind, those goals would become achievements, and I could do anything I put my mind to. Any obstacle in life is only as big as you allow it to be. It is not that you *cannot* do something, it is that you *will not*. Instead of "if," replace it with a word of certainty such as "when," "of course," or "yet." Lay the foundations to make your dreams a reality. If you take the first step, and keep going, soon you will be overlooking an amazing empire you have built.

I am not, by any means, saying it will be easy, but do not look behind you. Do not let your past be a burden. When your memories come to haunt you, remember they are only as real as you allow them to be. You are in control of your mind and the thoughts it produces. When your mind is being negative, remind it that you are not accepting invitations to harmful ways of thinking anymore.

It is easy to be an addict, feeling sorry for yourself. It is easy to make excuses and be a lifeless mind and body roaming among others who choose to be as pathetic as you are. Break the cycle and commit to being something better. When you do, pass it on to someone else. I did not get to where I am today by feeling sorry for the predicament I put myself in. In the end, everyone could not stand being around me. They all despised the person I had become. So, I became a person that people now want to be around. Those I hold close to my heart love and respect me. As a junkie, it was something that was hard to picture. Now, I cannot imagine my life any other way.

There are helpful tools for those who struggle, but you have what it takes within yourself. I can promise there are thousands of people in this world who have overcome the same things you are struggling with now, and they will be there to guide you on your journey if you seek a better way of living.

"I can do anything I want. And so can you."
-Frank, Donnie Darko

To The Affected Family

I have been on both sides of addiction. I have loved people who were plagued with it, while also being the cause of my family's suffering. When I am asked to speak, especially for a prevention organization started by parents, I am asked similar questions:

How do I know if my child is using drugs?

My mother said she had a "gut feeling" much before my behavior changed. Drug users change their entire personality. If you feel your children have been more distant, defiant, or rebellious, I recommend monitoring their behavior.

Addicts usually steal–watch your cash and belongings closely. There are a few physical elements you can look for as well.

Amphetamine users will have enlarged pupils. Their behavior is frantic and compulsive, moving and talking quickly and obsessing over simple things, such as focusing on the tiniest specks on the floor during routine household cleaning. Amphetamine users can be manic, aggressive, show rapid weight loss and may have sores and scabs from picking at their skin, sometimes called tweaking.

Opiate users have very small pupils, almost as small as a pin, hence the term "pinned pupils." Stealing is common for many users. Opiate addicts lack attention skills. They may be very tired to the point of nodding off. In my personal opinion, opiate addicts have a pasty sort of look to them.

I think overall, as a parent you know your child, and if you sense something is wrong, you are most likely correct.

What should I do if my child is using?
There is nothing you can do to stop them! As a parent, this is difficult to accept. In my time, the only thing I have ever seen to be effective is to cut them off completely. Let them see what life as a drug addict is like. *Kick them out!* The only reason I sought help is because I had nothing left. No one to help me or feel sorry for me. I had to make things work, and I knew my parents were not going to let me come back home. I became desperate enough to want to save my own life.

Here is how I look at it: If your kids are using, and you let them stay at home, you are basically telling them you accept their behavior; and it is all right if they continue to act this way. By giving them a place to live, free food, a shower and many other privileges, you are not punishing them in the least. If they cannot accept your house rules, then they should not live there. It took me sleeping on the floors of my friends' homes, and begging to use people's showers to realize it would have been much easier to quit using and have a place to live. I know if my parents continued to give me all of the things I wanted, I never would have stopped. Using drugs is serious, so the punishment should be equally as serious. Do not *ever* enable an addict.

This is the defense I get from parents when I tell them my opinion: If I kick them out, what if they die? Or end up in jail, or end up missing, or trafficked into prostitution or slavery? How am I supposed to sleep at night, knowing my kid is on the streets?

You are not going to sleep for a while. I know because my mom did not. She cried every night and waited in terror for the possible phone call that I had lost my life. When I got sober, I came to the drastic conclusion that not all addicts were going to make it, but there was nothing anyone could do to stop them. If someone does not want to get clean and refuses to get help, whether they overdosed at home or on the street; either way they were going to die. There is a theory that every junkie has to hit rock bottom. In my opinion, that is true to a point. I believe there is such a thing as an emotional rock bottom.

When I decided to enter treatment, it was because something soul-shattering happened. I remember the moment clearly. I was getting ready to take a shower, and I wondered when the last time I showered was; and I felt ashamed. Then, for the first time in months, I finally got a good look at myself in the mirror. I was barely 100 pounds, and I looked sick. My eyes had heavy bags, and my skin was pasty and corpse-like. My hair was falling out. But more than anything, I did not recognize the girl in the mirror. I did not know her at all. She had no personality or emotions. She was basically only alive physically. There was no denying that I was completely dead inside. For a moment, I thought of my family and broke into tears when I felt my heart break, knowing they could not love me anymore. I was completely and entirely alone, and it was of my own doing.

I listened while a girl was fending off a rape. I have been raped three times. I sat in a room with overdose victims—most likely dead—and used heroin right next to them. And I killed my unborn child. None of these things weighed heavily enough to make me want to change or to make me recognize what I had turned into.

Everyone's realization is different. The longer junkies are enabled, it is less likely they will come to that understanding. Some of us will make it out of addiction alive, others will not. Cutting off their financial and emotional ties to you is taking care of yourself. If you are not the one using drugs, why should you be punished? Remember, as I have said time and time again, using drugs is a choice. This is what they have chosen to be, chosen to do. Let their decision cost them. If addicts cannot find whatever is left of their soul, it is impossible someone else will find it for them.

Perhaps these suggestions seem inhumane and unfair. Maybe you are thinking I do not know what I am talking about because I am not a parent. Perhaps you are right, but I am a sober junkie. I carried this burden for five years and pulled out of it. I know what did, and did not, work while I was using.

When people ask what made me get clean, I tell them it started with my dad telling me to pack up my shit and get out. I can assure you I never thought my parents would kick me out. I love my family with every ounce of my being. I had betrayed and abused them, and I paid the consequence. Today I know how horrid it is to live life as a heroin addict and alcoholic. I know what awaits me if the day ever comes that I choose to go back to the disgusting life I know so well. I also know that having a relationship with my family is a privilege. They do not owe me their love. I know how painful it is to be ostracized without it. That is the heartbreaking lesson every addict must figure out. It was only as I stood in the shadow of death, destroyed and alone, that I was able to choose life. I decided to re-create myself into something beautiful, rather than broken.

To Those Who Find Sobriety

If you have made it past the detox, then the worst of the physical damage is over. Regaining your emotions is going to be interesting and frustrating. Remember, you have everything you need to stay sober within yourself. Be stern, and make a commitment that going back to your habit will not be an option, no matter what.

When I saw Ro for the first time after I got clean, she could not stop crying. Her sadness agonized me. I was confused, rationalizing she should be happy I was sober. But she finally explained that the very idea of her having to go to my funeral was devastating. It was worse that I had chosen to be so close to death, that my choice was to force her to watch my lifeless shape being lowered into a six-foot-deep hole, ensuring she would never see me again.

I think it was hard for her to comprehend how I could choose to take myself away from her. I recall seeing her when I was heavily into my addiction and hearing her scream from the angriest part of her soul for the return of her sister. It is hard to believe I hurt her and the rest of my family so much.

In the beginning of my sobriety, when I questioned going back to drugs, I thought of my sister. Her eyes welling with tears amid her sobs. I thought of my mom looking around as she drove home from work, hoping to see any sign that would tell her I was still breathing. I thought of my dad's sighs and his tired eyes filled with disappointment. I thought of how my brothers were ashamed to answer questions about me. Who the hell did I think I was to cause this pain? That I would sooner give my life to heroin than make the right choice to end my family's suffering?

Maybe the truth was I did not value myself, nor did I care if I woke up in the morning. Maybe I lacked the quality of seeing importance in my life, but I saw value in theirs. I have learned to respect that the right choices will help myself, my family and many others in this world. I have a voice today, whether I wanted one or not, and I must do what I can to keep it.

I am so very blessed I did not lose my life to addiction, and I have no desire to see if I can be so lucky twice. My life has purpose; for that, I am thankful. With that said, the best way to show my family I value their happiness is to be a better person. That is not possible when I am high.

I recommend you turn a deaf ear to the voices in your head. When they howl that they want substances or you are in need, tell them to fuck off. Break free of the insanity you have created to act as your reality. Be everything you ever dreamed of becoming. If you waste time feeling sorry for yourself and having a bad attitude, you are only holding yourself back. Change your perception. Let the judgments of others pass you by. No one matters but you and the ones you love. You will grow and better judge who is disposable, and who is not.

You are able to be anything you want if you give yourself the chance. Drugs and alcohol are irrelevant to life. They are as useless as a pen in math class. Do not set up an obstacle that is futile. There is a whole world you have yet to see through eyes that have never been used before. Allow yourself to surrender. Break down, fall apart. When we are at our worst, we find an opportunity to start over.

I hear of people relapsing and struggling to get sober. It is this elementary and only as difficult as you want it to be. You are in control of your life. Once you refrain from substances long enough, staying clean is as natural as breathing. Make it happen. Using simply is not an option. No matter what the circumstances.

In order to be productive, we must continue our growth at all times. Commit to being strong and dependable. If, at first, you do not believe in yourself, find someone who does and learn from them. May you hold the world in the palm of your hand. May you have sobriety as naturally as the air filling your lungs. May you never look behind you, and work hard to build a world beyond your wildest dreams. Make your addiction your past, not your present. May you never doubt, for even a single moment, the strength that comes from within.

About The Author: Tommy Zee

Tommy Zee grew up in Newbury Park, California. Early studies of authors in elementary school inspired her love for writing. Edgar Allan Poe was the main inspiration during those times. Tommy finds motivation to write because of her desire for everyone to find something to relate to and have a voice in the world. When she isn't writing, Tommy enjoys studying different artists and writers. Her favorite to study is Salvador Dali with Vincent Van Gough as a very close runner up. "It was only as I stood in the shadow of death, destroyed and alone, that I was able to choose life," Tommy bravely says in her biography "Junkie." She shares her story with us because she wants us all to know the dangers of using drugs and that the decisions we make do have consequences. Tommy is currently working on ideas for her next book and consistently writing on her blog which can be found at www.boneyhandblog.wordpress.com. You can follow Tommy on her "author" Facebook page, "Junkie" Facebook page or on Twitter to stay up to date on any events, works in progress or advice from Tommy.

Read where Tommy found the inspiration for the cover of "Junkie" on the next page!

When I entered rehab, it was like starting at a new school. My peers made me anxious, not only were they strangers, but junkie criminals like me. I was terrified of detox after hearing people curse their experiences. I questioned if I was ready. The second day into it I wanted to die. I couldn't stop sweating. I was shaking like I was afflicted with Parkinson's, and I was too fatigued to function. I showed up at my group and did my best to participate. One of the other girls who had been sober for a while was showing her before-and-after photos. On the left, she was high; on the right, 90 days sober. My counselor studied it. He told her how amazing the transformation showed up in her eyes. On the left, they were disconnected and hollow. On the right, they were confident and alive.

I had been too ashamed for months to look in the mirror. When I got home, I sorted through my photos and found the same disconnection in every picture. My eyes were dead. How had I never noticed before? For the first time in a few days, my body seemed calm. I was due for another dose of Suboxone but postponed it. In that moment, I realized I was sober for the first time in five years. I went into the bathroom to see what the sober me looked like. Skinny, sick, extremely tired but alive. For the first time in half-a-decade, I didn't look corpse-like. I was being resurrected. With every horrible withdrawal symptom, my body was reviving, functioning more like it was designed to.

My eyes were warm. When I was using, they were a deep, dirt-like matte brown. Now they had an amber tint. Like a fire igniting inside. They were reconnecting to all my human emotions. I ran into my room to capture the moment. I made this image the screensaver on my phone, to remind me at all times that I was working hard to stay sober and alive. I became comfortable with facing myself and really coming to understand this person. The first time I connected with the sober me was in that photo. From then on, everyone I knew and loved seemed to connect with me in some way or another. It kept me motivated to stay sober. To keep the fire burning.

Reviews of Junkie

Junkie is an astonishing look at the depths of depravity endured by somebody in the grips of addiction. The lengths at which a person is willing to push themselves to chase that unsasiable urge, and the horrors that go along with it. While also showing that we who suffer from addiction can overcome it, and live a life we never believed possible.

- Tommy Zee paints a perfect picture of her life as a junkie, and how she rose above addictions that ran her life for years, coming out the other end stronger than even she possibly ever imagined. -

I don't think I have sat still for as long as I did to read this book. My ADHD disappeared after the first chapter. Tommy writes this book almost as a warning to others of what NOT to do in their life, and I believe also to give hope to those who have already made some of the same choices. This book was inspiring for me, having gone down some of the same roads as the author, I found myself getting lost in the book. It was a mixture of nostalgia, sympathy, apathy, and joy. As a man, I don't like to admit too often to crying, but I caught myself choking back tears (of joy) actually at one point in the book. Others may find tears of sadness falling down their cheeks while reading this book. You feel her pain, struggles and agony, and then feel like you have conquered your own demons after finishing the book, feeling like you can go out and accomplish anything that is brought before you. This is an amazing book whether you are in the disease of addiction or not, whether you know someone or not. This is a book ultimately of defeating the odds and triumphing over evil. I recommend this book to anyone, however I do believe it will be best received from people directly or indirectly dealing with addiction.

Other Great Works By Tommy Zee!!

THE GAME WHOLEHEARTED

TOMMY ZEE

Here is your secret weapon to dating! The dating world is difficult to survive in. We often get discouraged, or frustrated. This book will help keep you from wasting your time with the wrong types of guys, and help you figure out which type is best for you. It will help you determine what type of guy you are dating from the start. This way you can easily decide if the relationship is worth continuing, or not. This book is formatted like a dictionary, this way you can skip to the type of guy you think you are dating. It can also be read all the way through so you are armed with the knowledge of all that is out there, with some self-help tips at the end. It's a helpful guide for all your dating endeavors!

Pick up your copy today on Amazon!

Made in the USA
Lexington, KY
15 March 2016